Basic Skills Workbook

Letters • Numbers • Shapes • Colors

866-451-5600
www.PreschoolPrepCo.com
P.O. Box 1159, Danville CA 94526

This book features all of the characters from the award winning Preschool Prep Series™ DVDs.

Meet the Letters™
Meet the Numbers™
Meet the Shapes™
Meet the Colors™

Created by
Kathy Oxley

Edited by
Peggy Valenzuela

Illustrated by
Emmanuel Acevedo, Lewis Jacobs, Derrick Dawson
Sherwin Rosario and Nick Trujillo

Preschool Prep Company®
P.O. Box 1159 Danville, CA 94526
www.PreschoolPrepCo.com
1-866-451-5600

Printed in China

Table of Contents

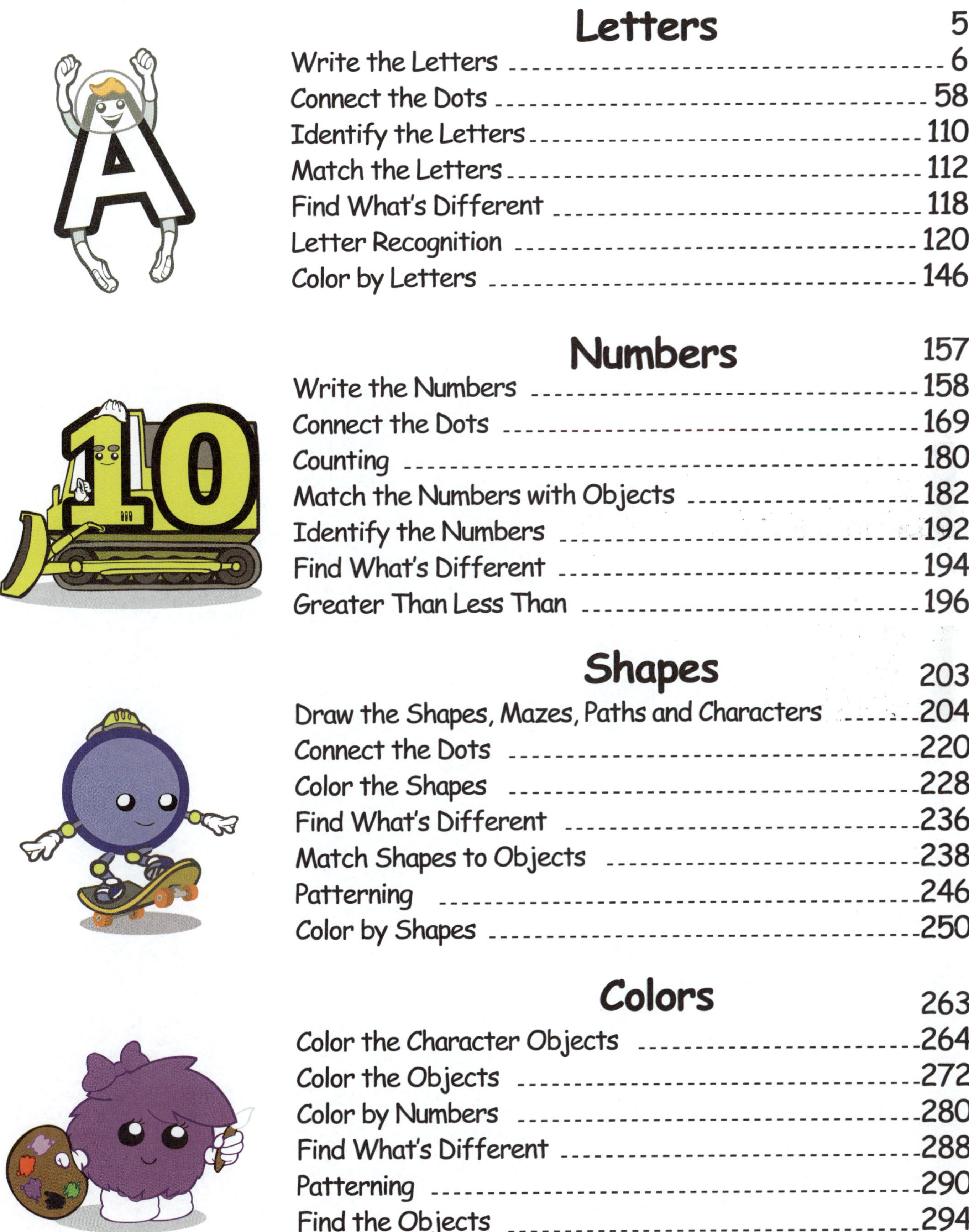

Meet the Letters™

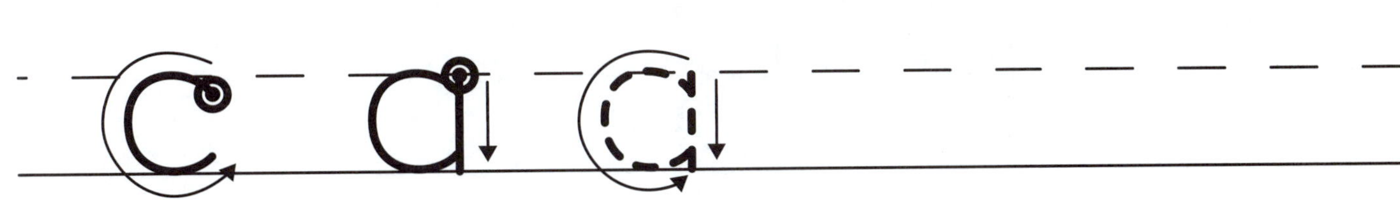

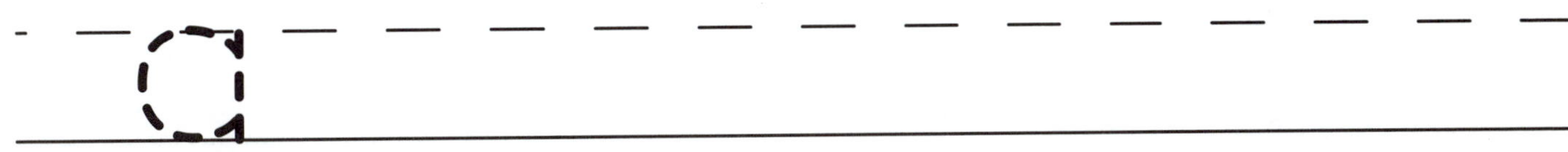

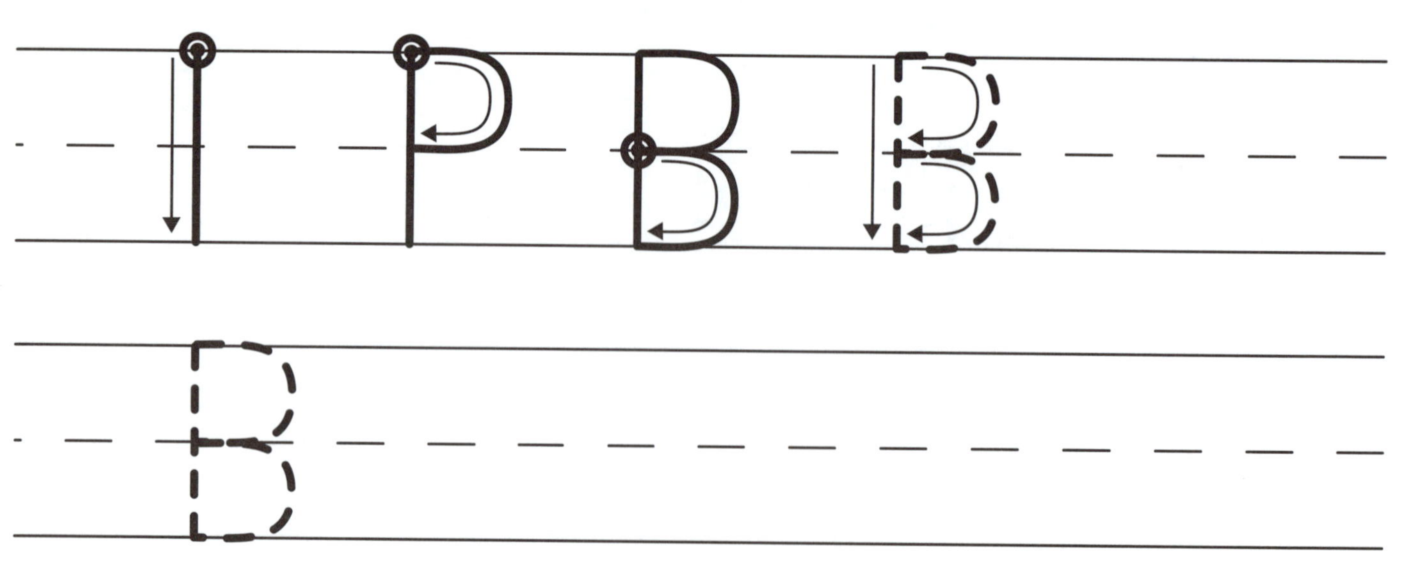

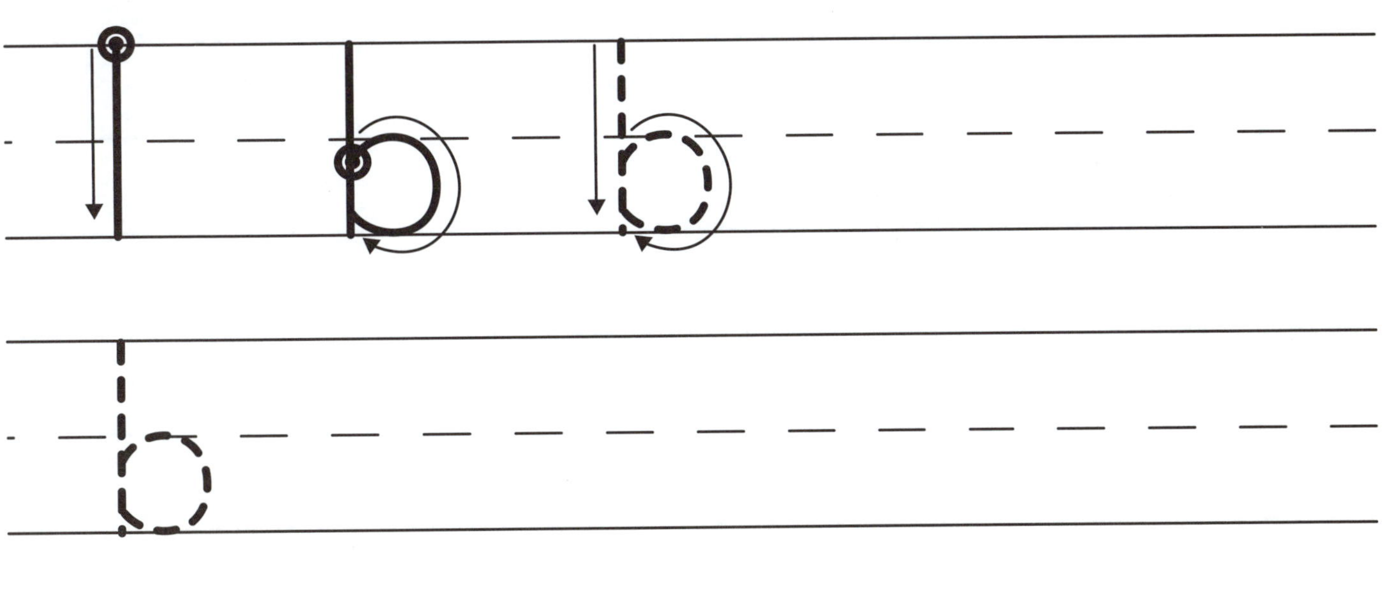

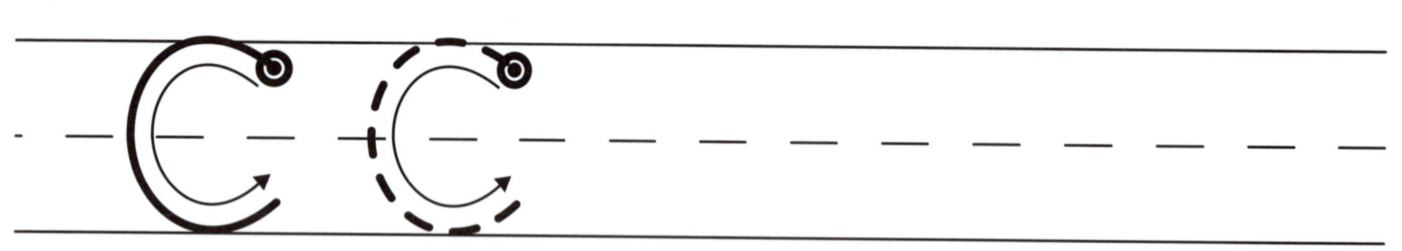

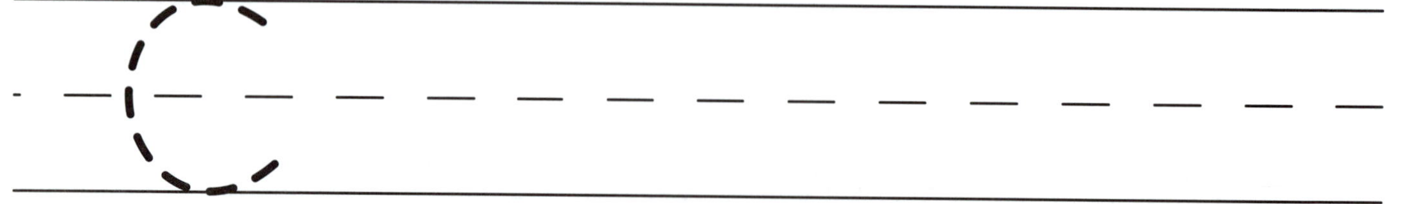

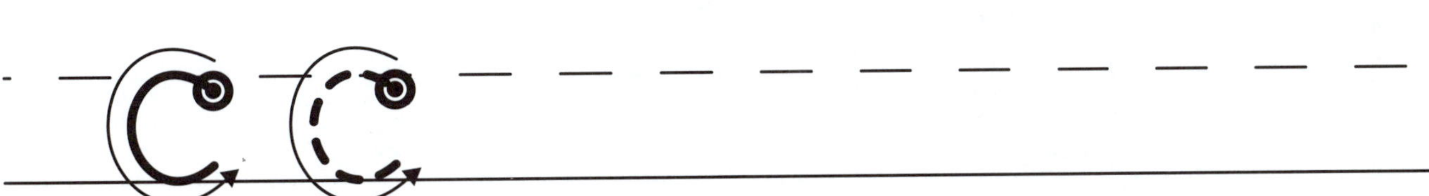

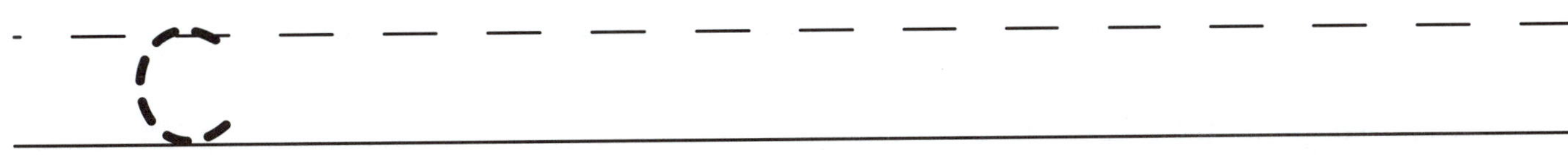

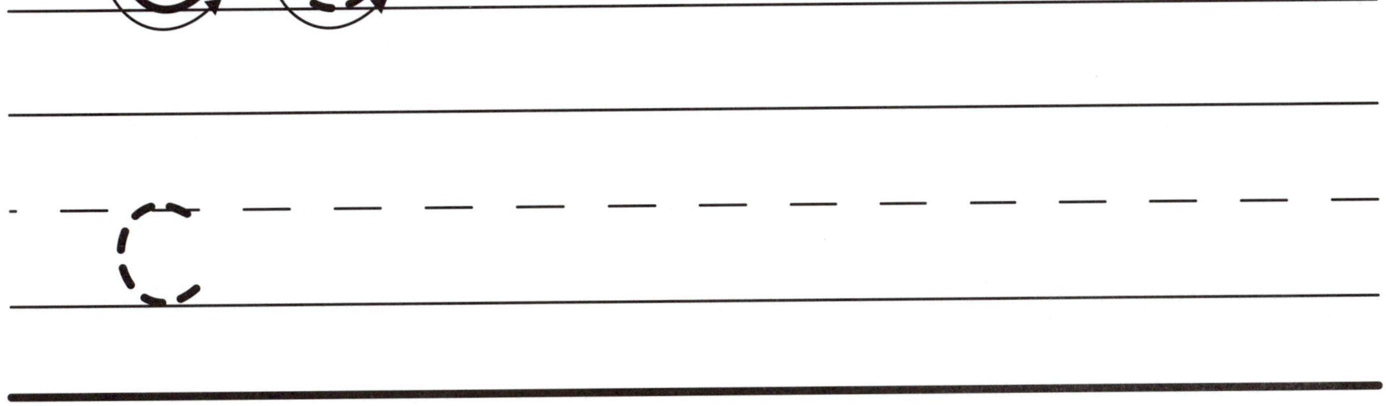

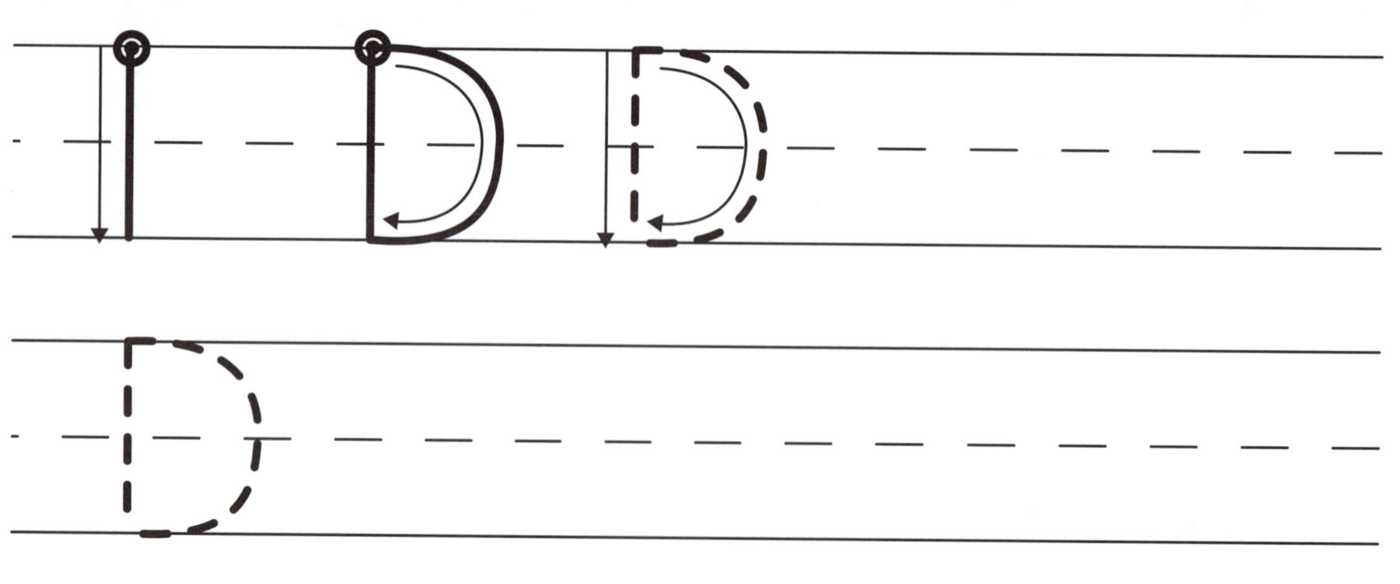

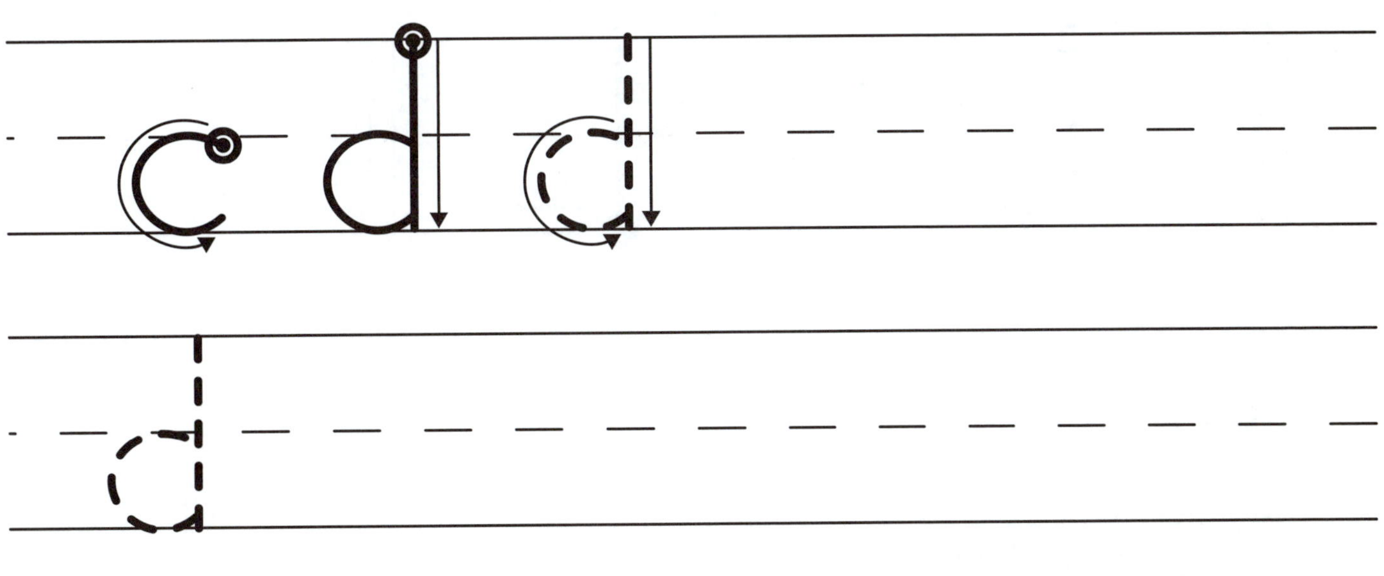

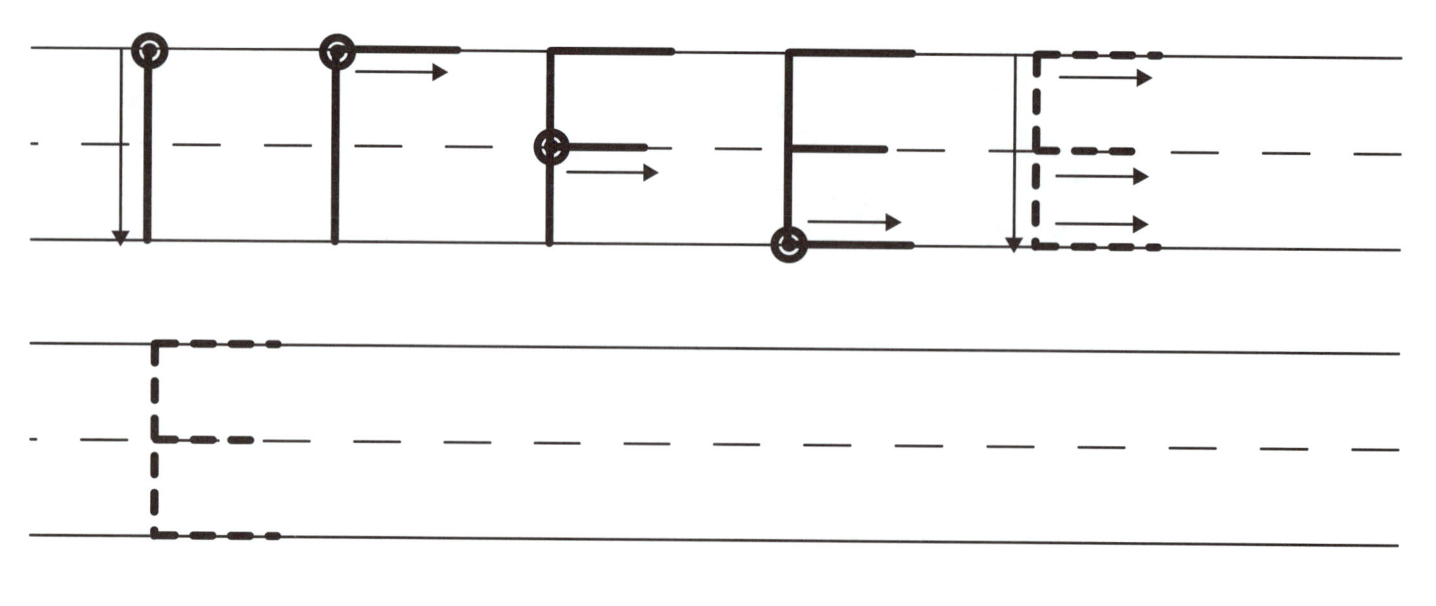

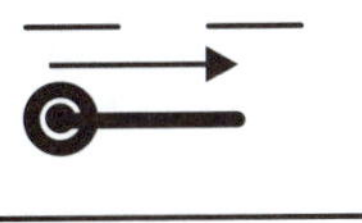

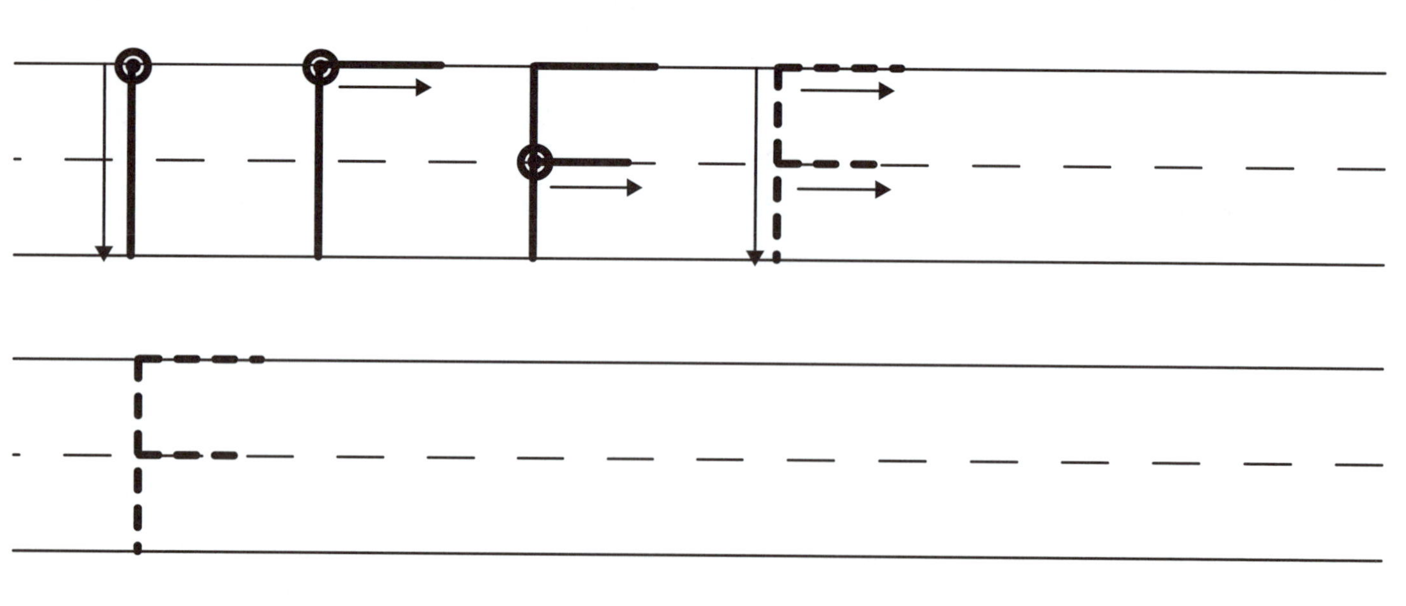

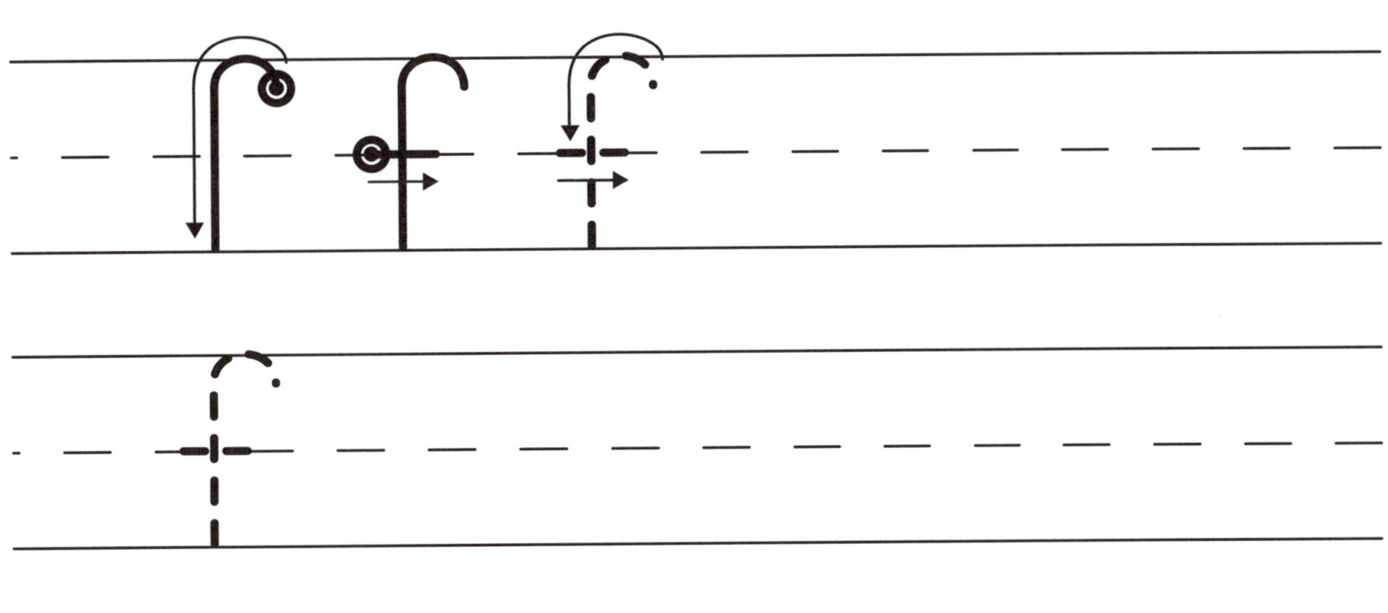

c g g
g

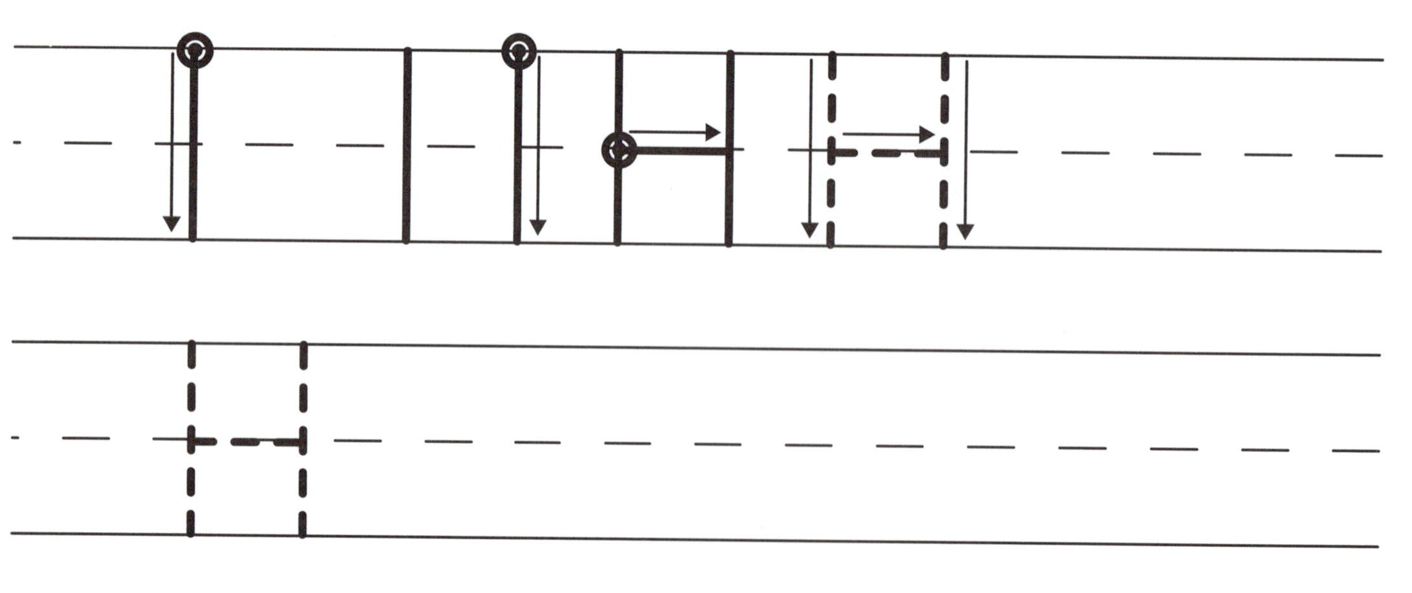

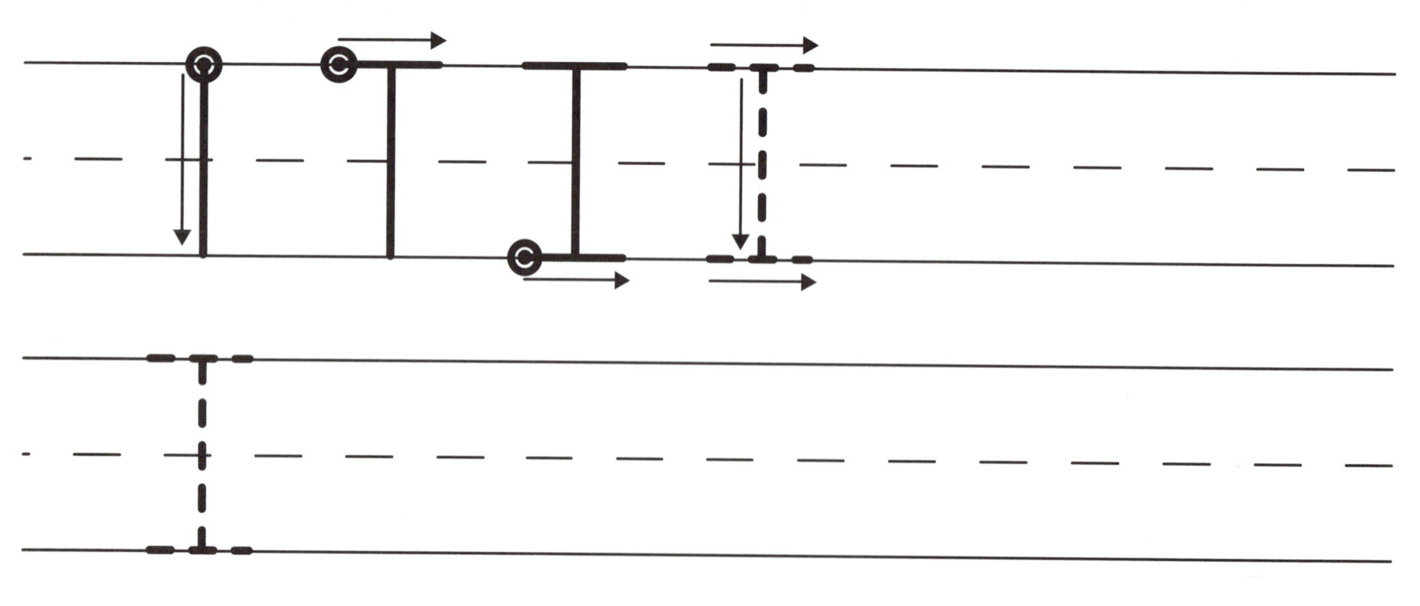

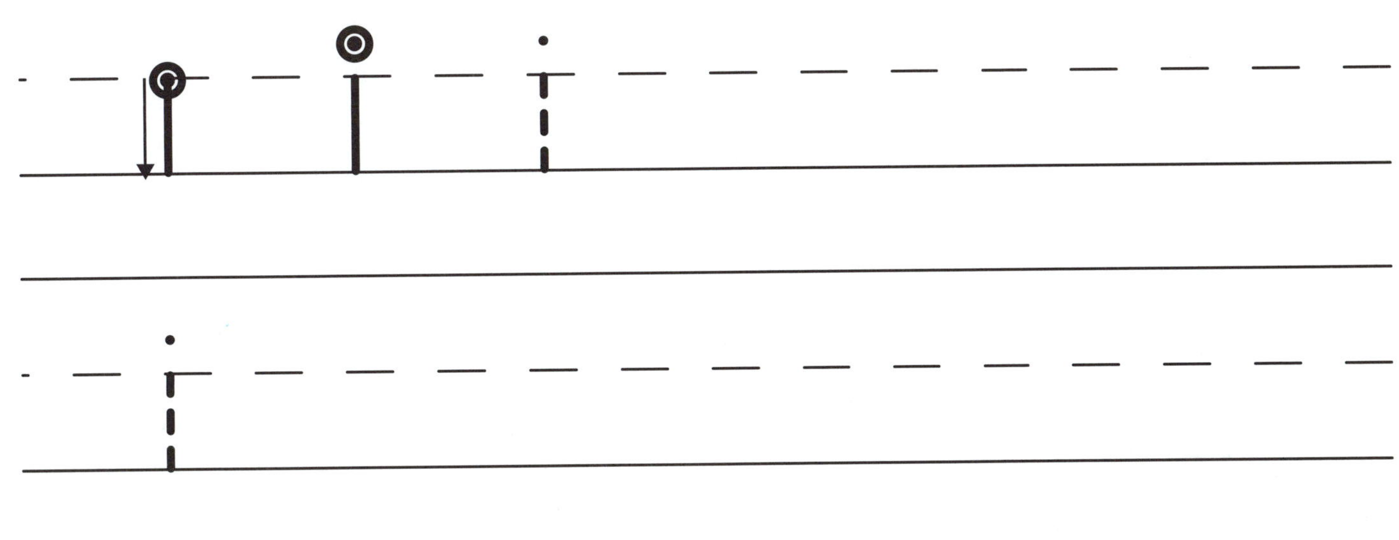

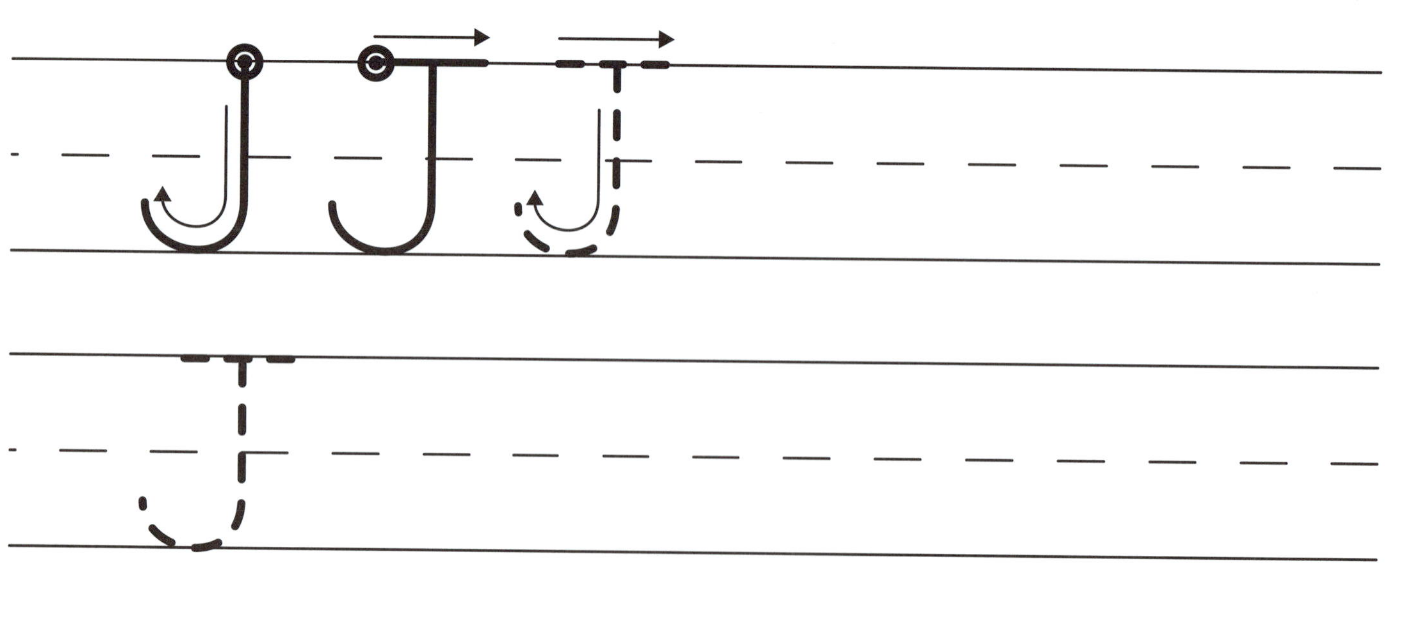

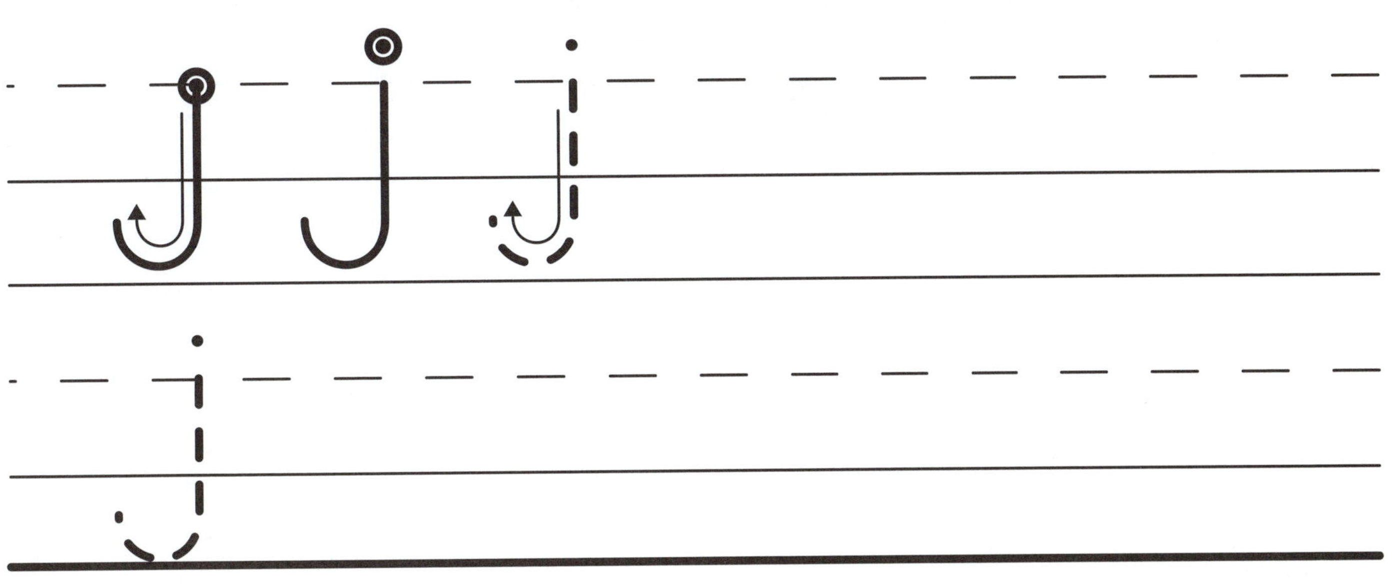
J J j
j

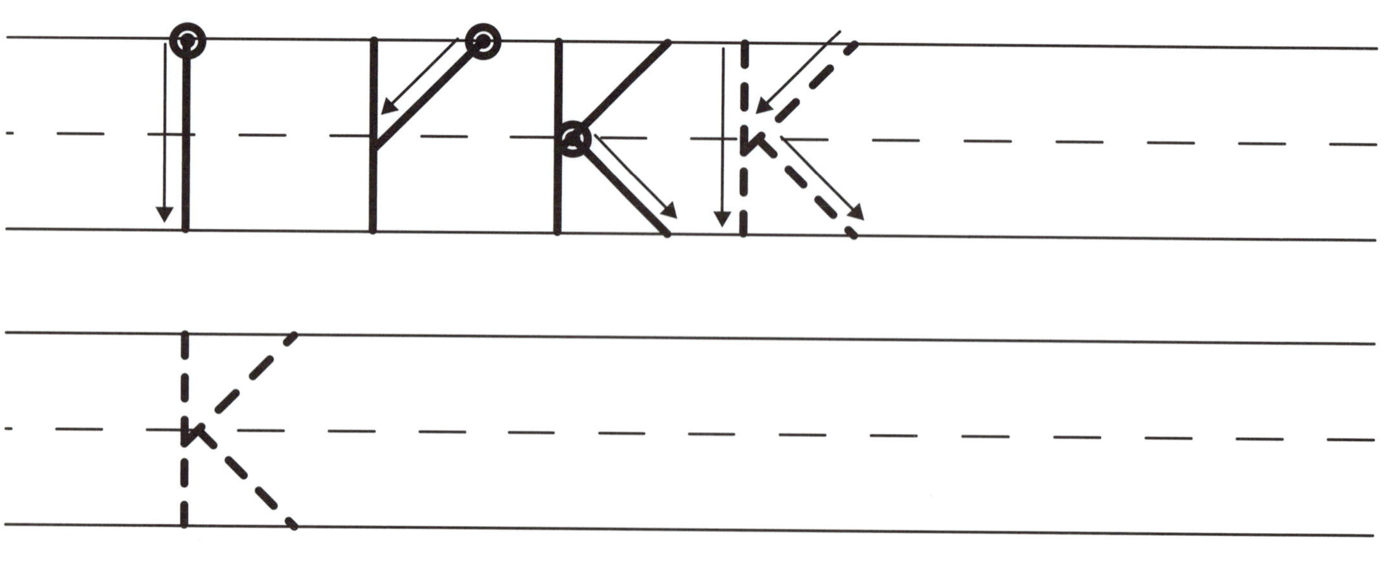

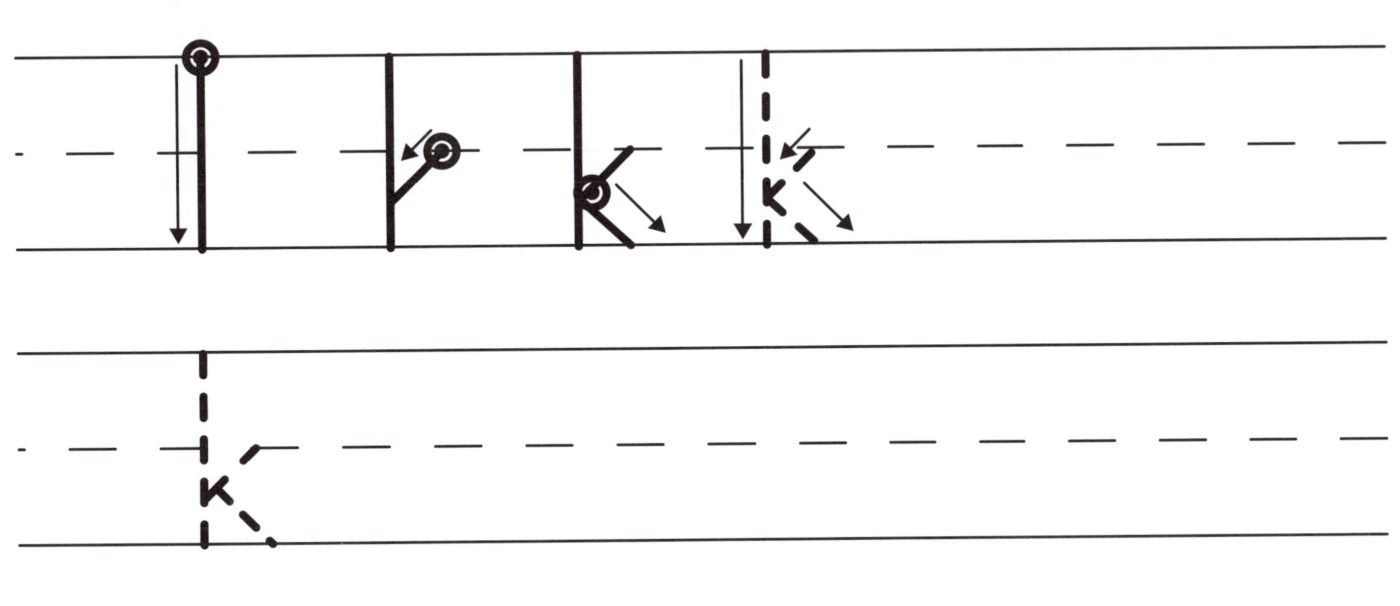

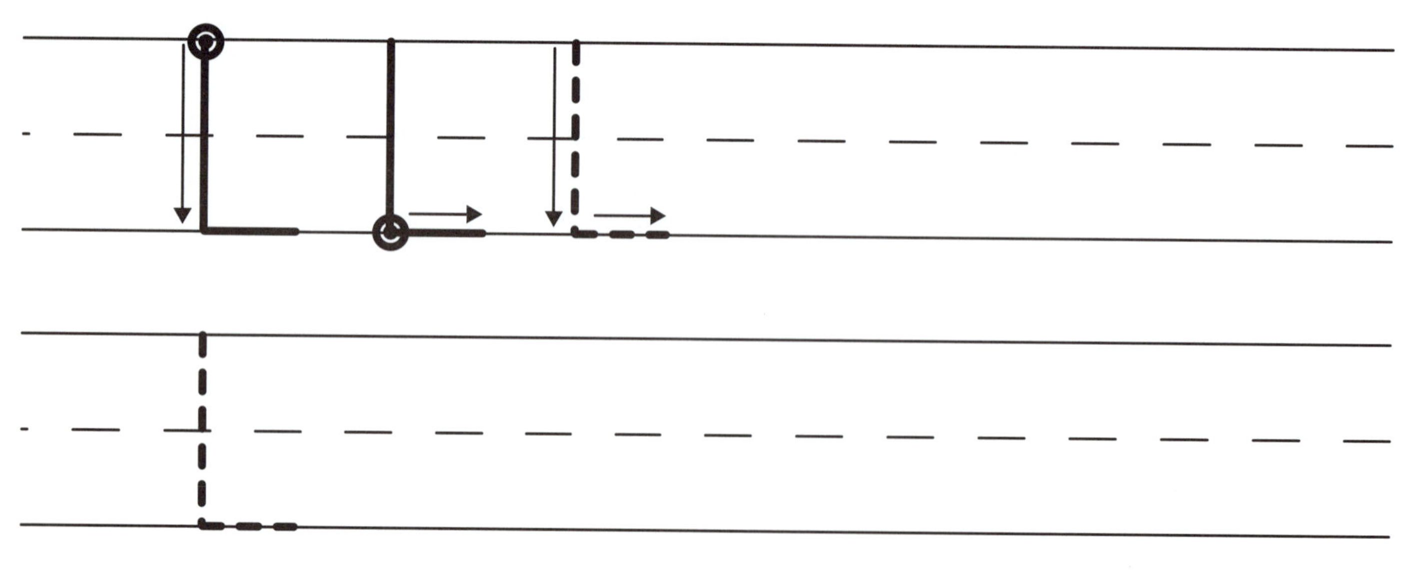

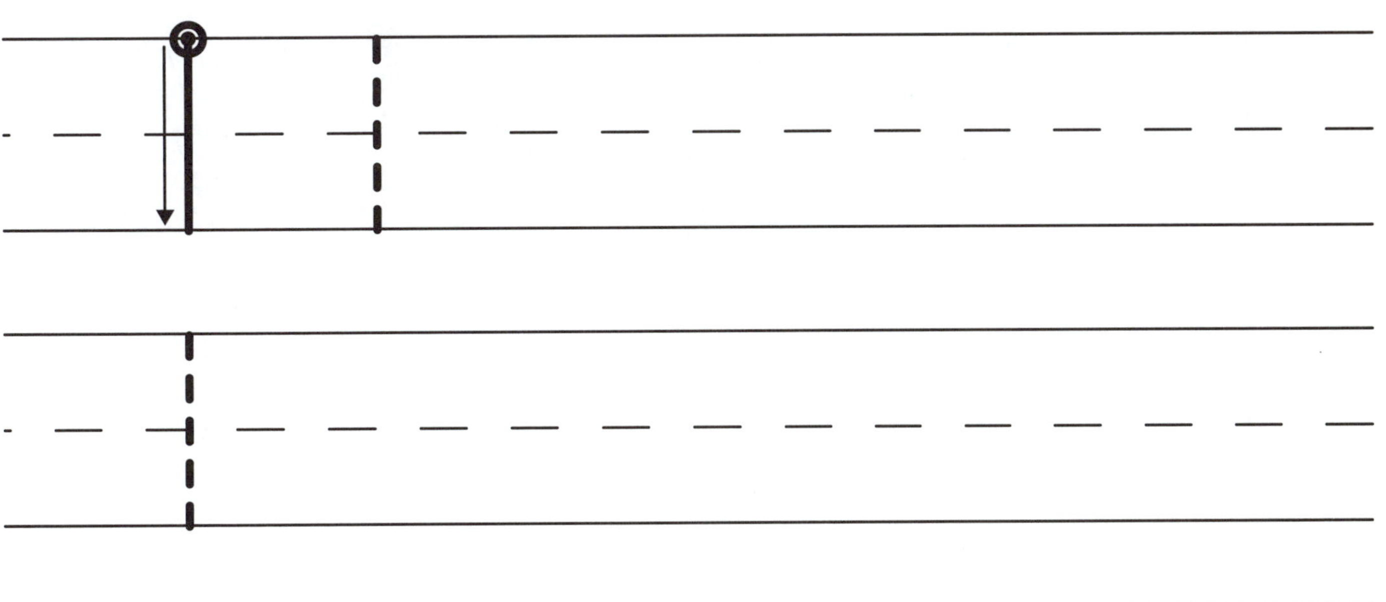

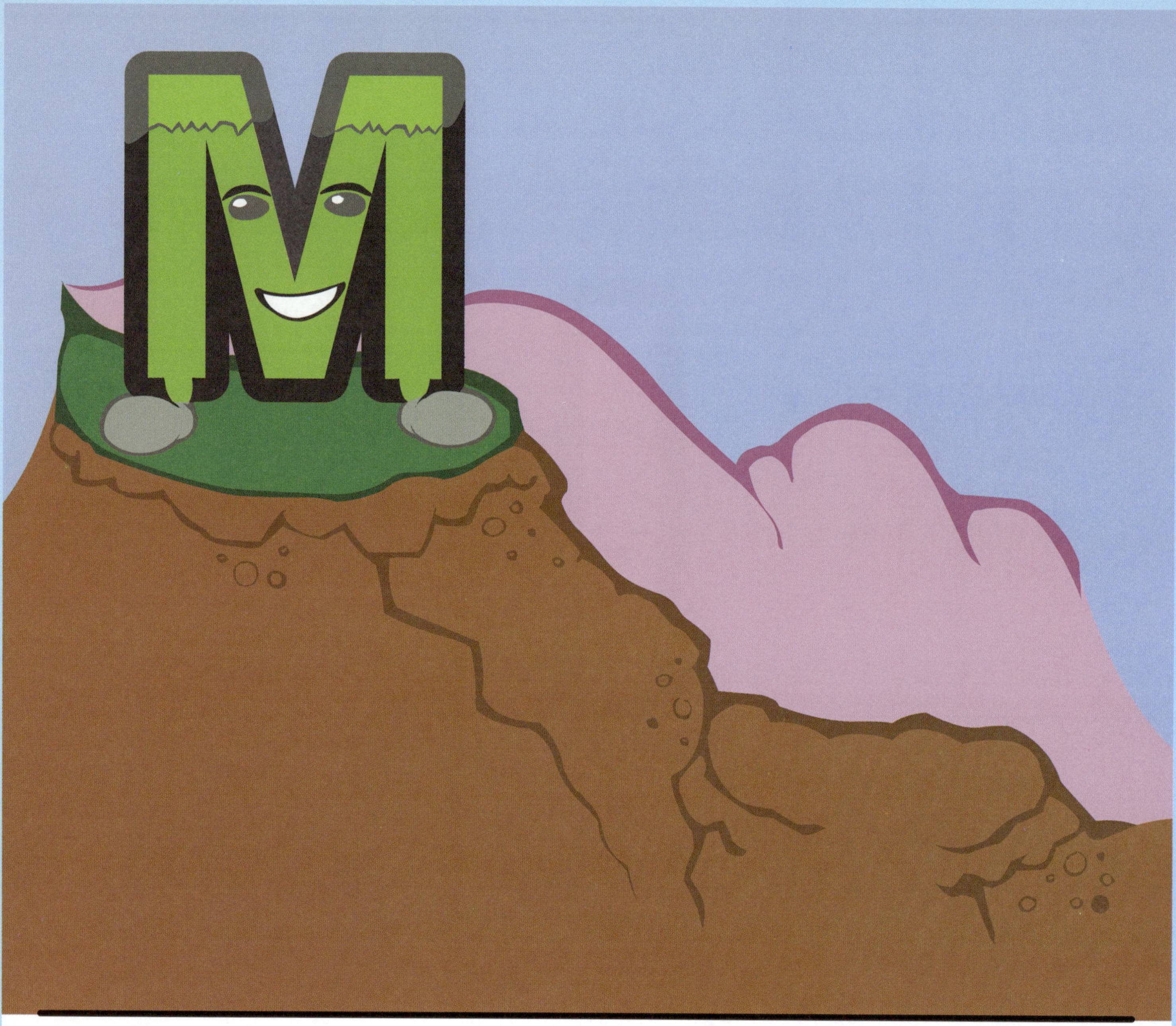

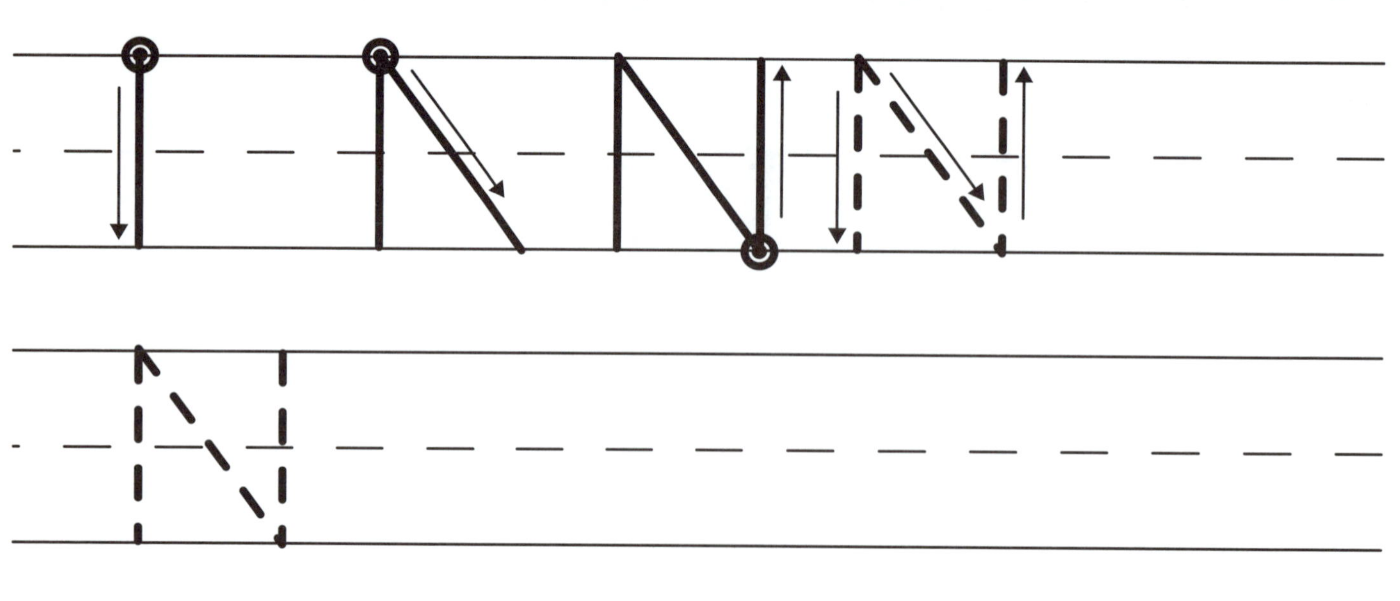

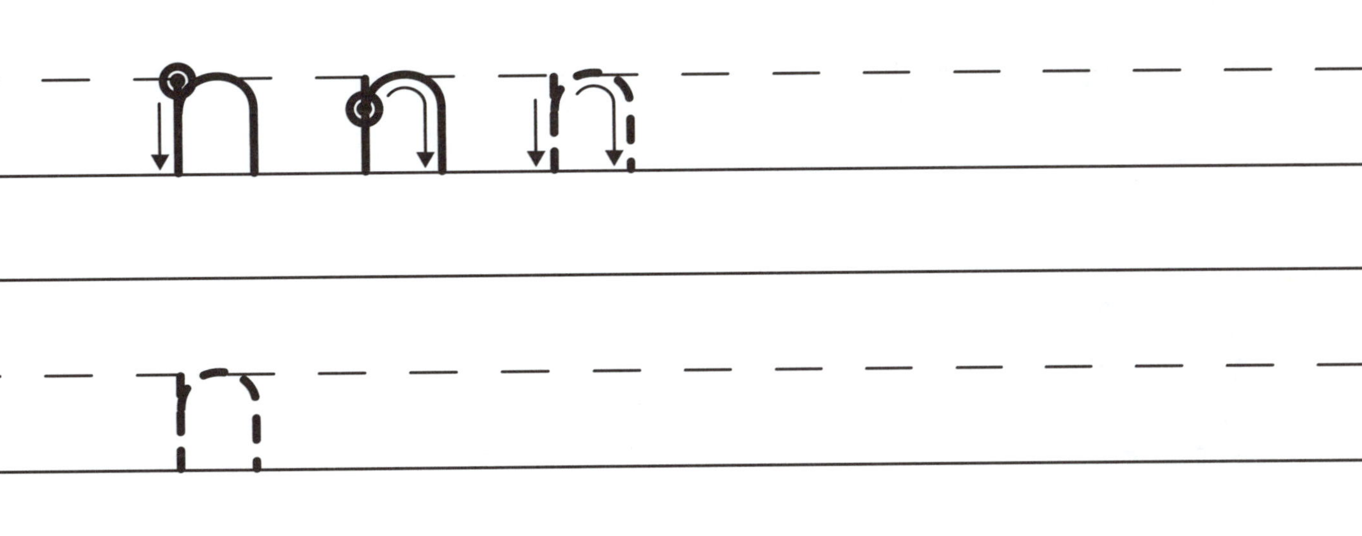
n n n
n

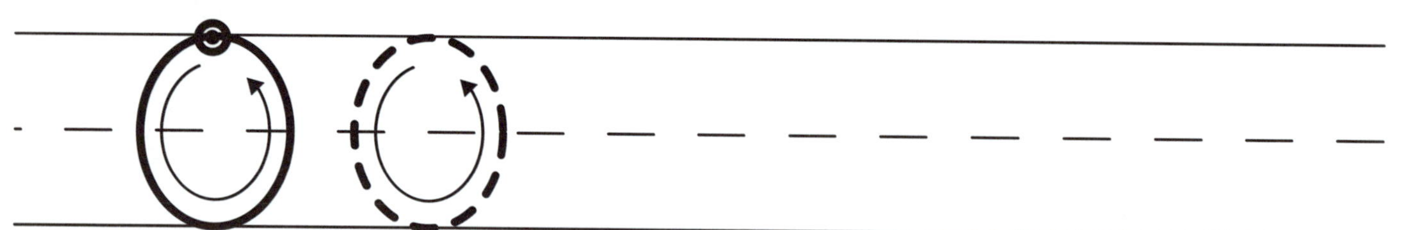

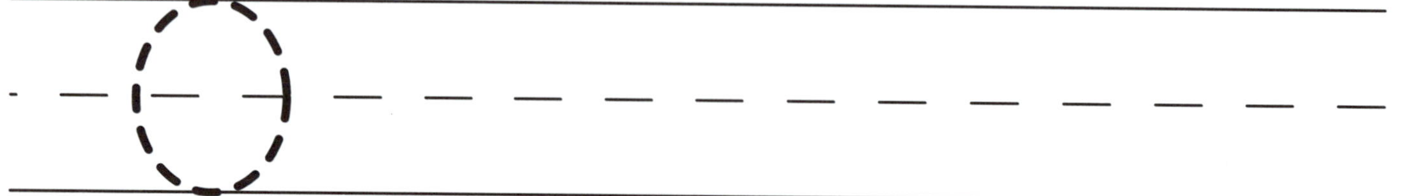

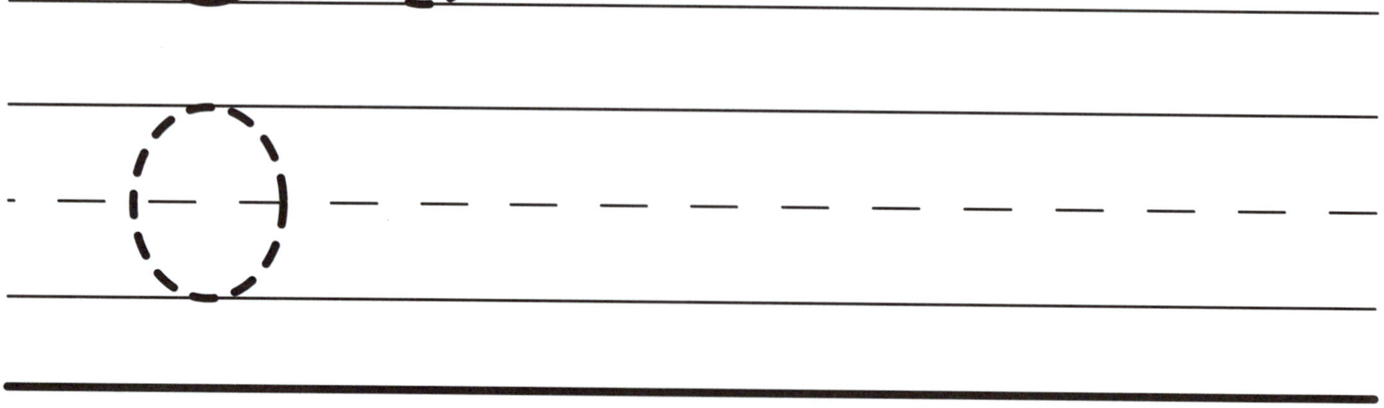

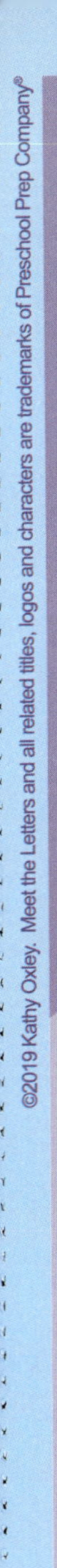

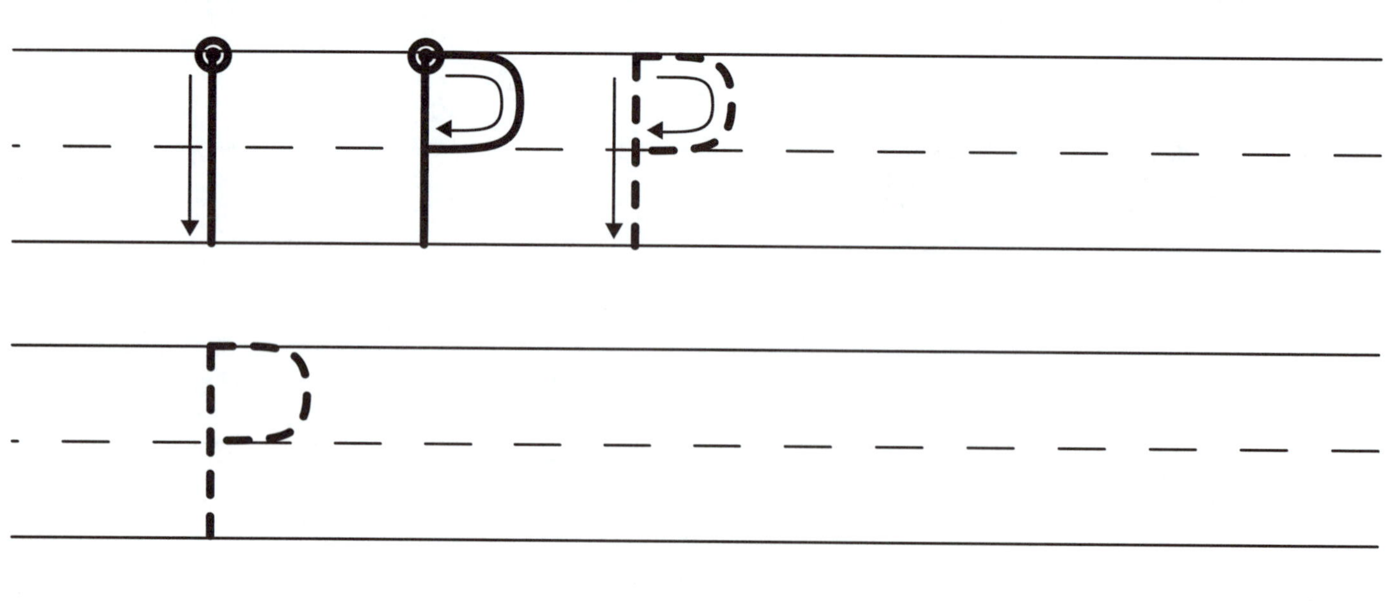

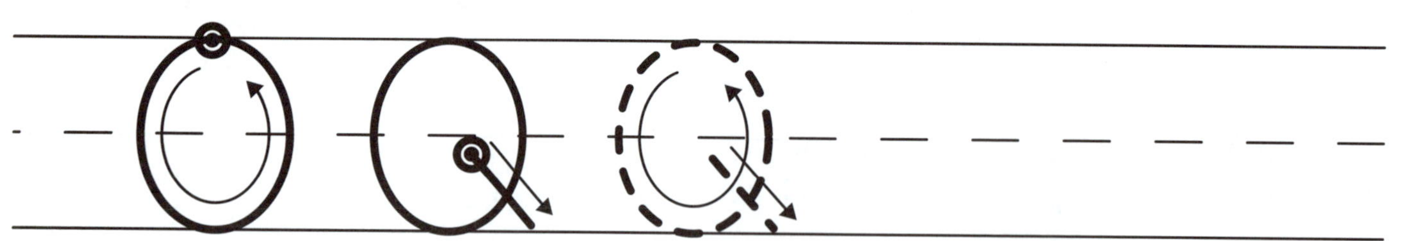

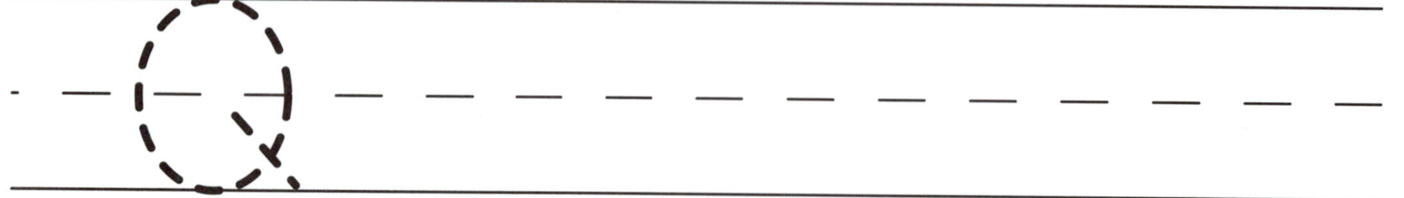

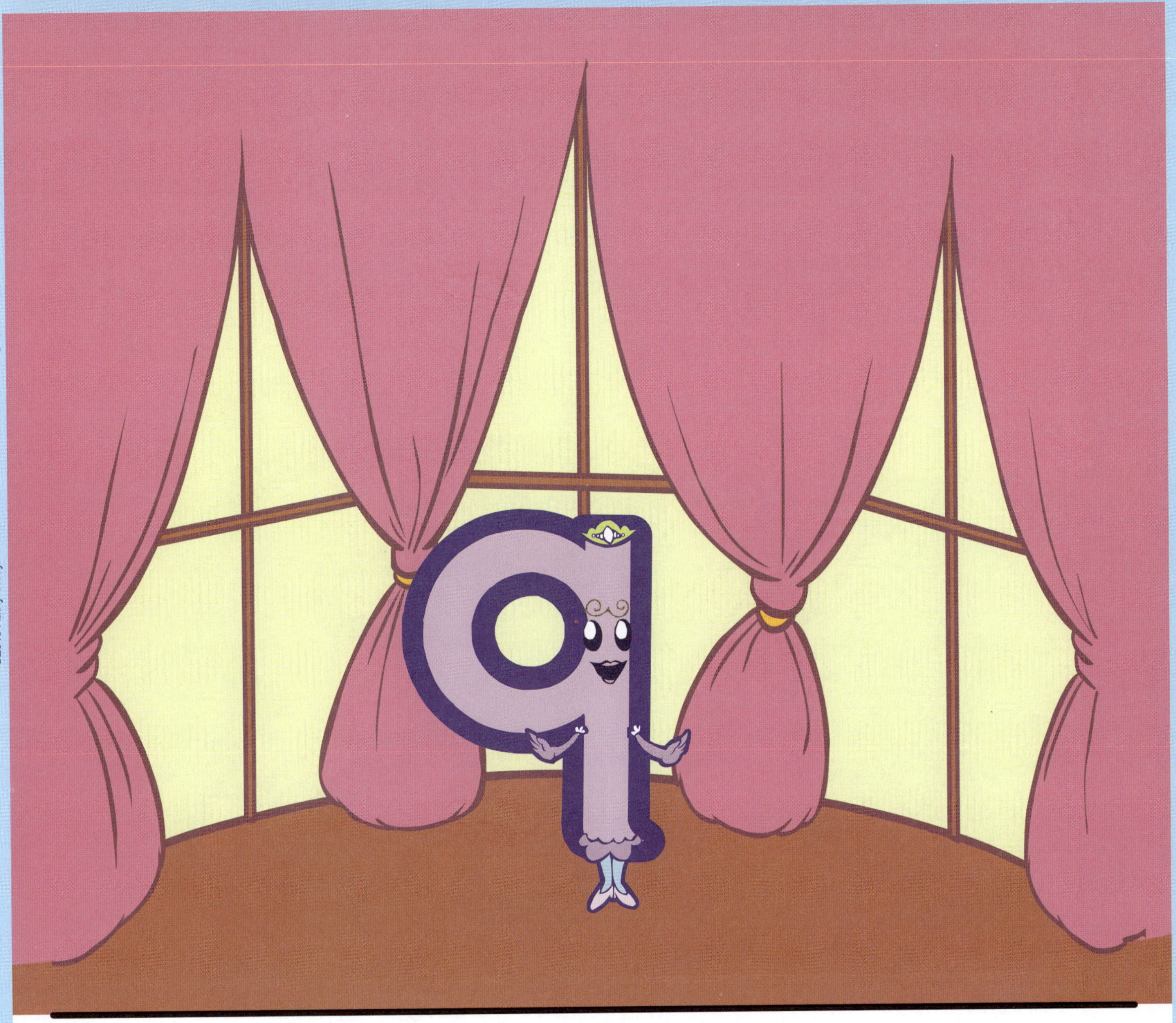

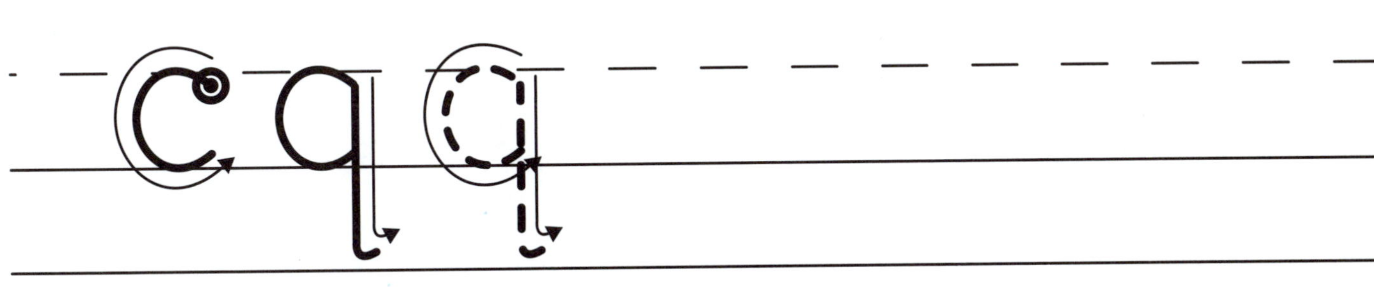
c q q

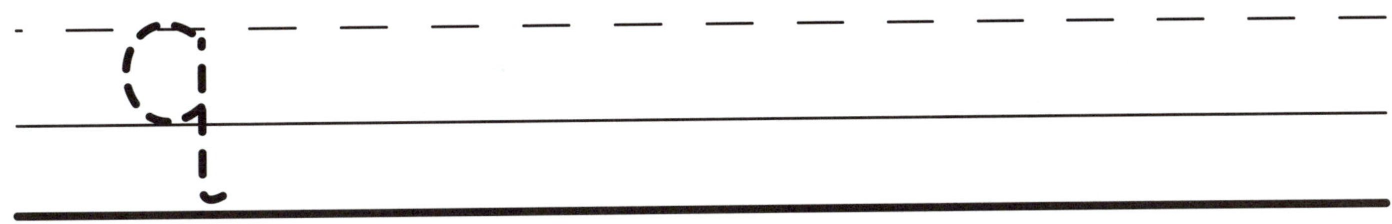
q

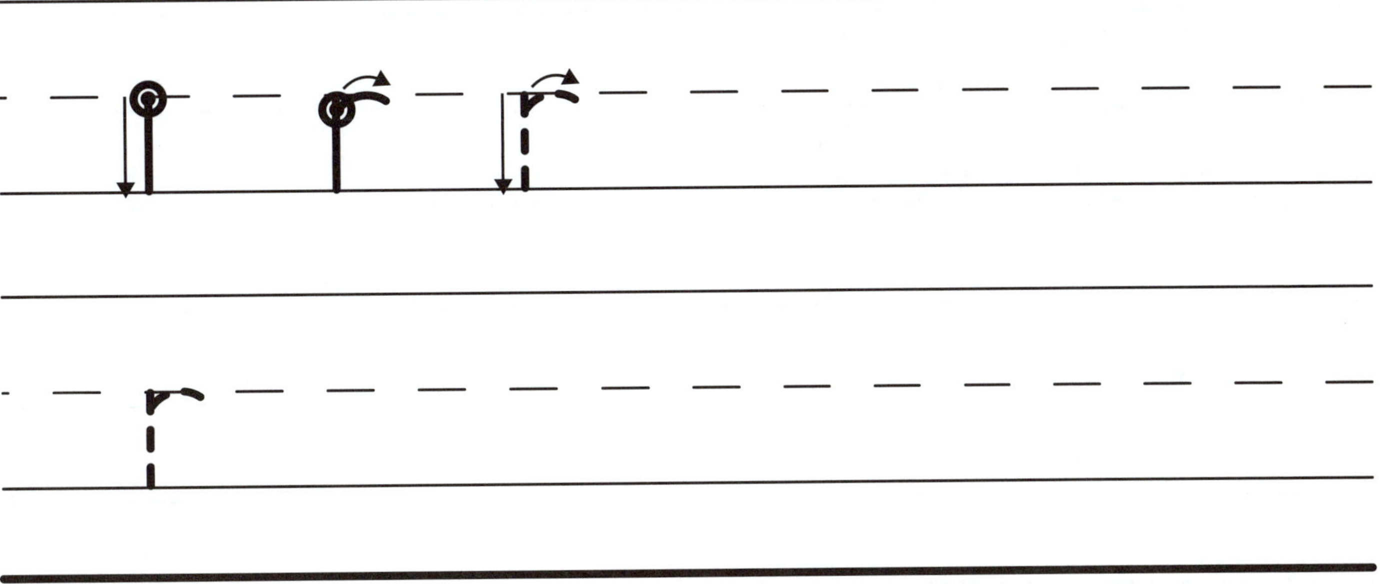

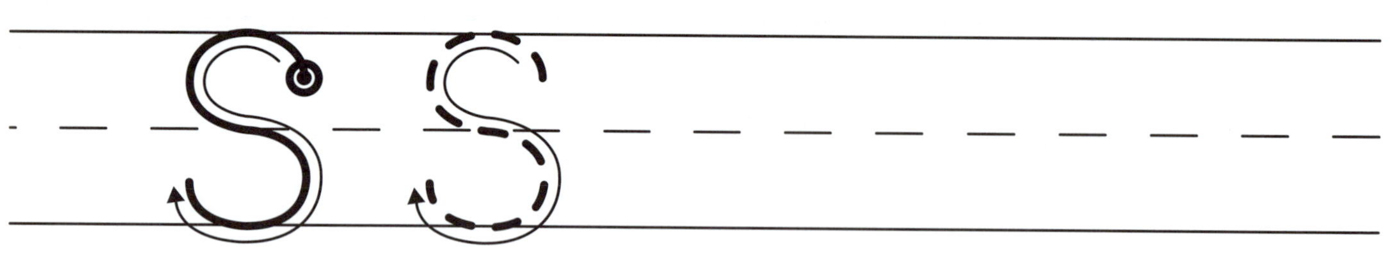

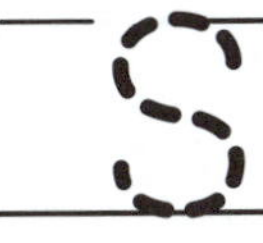

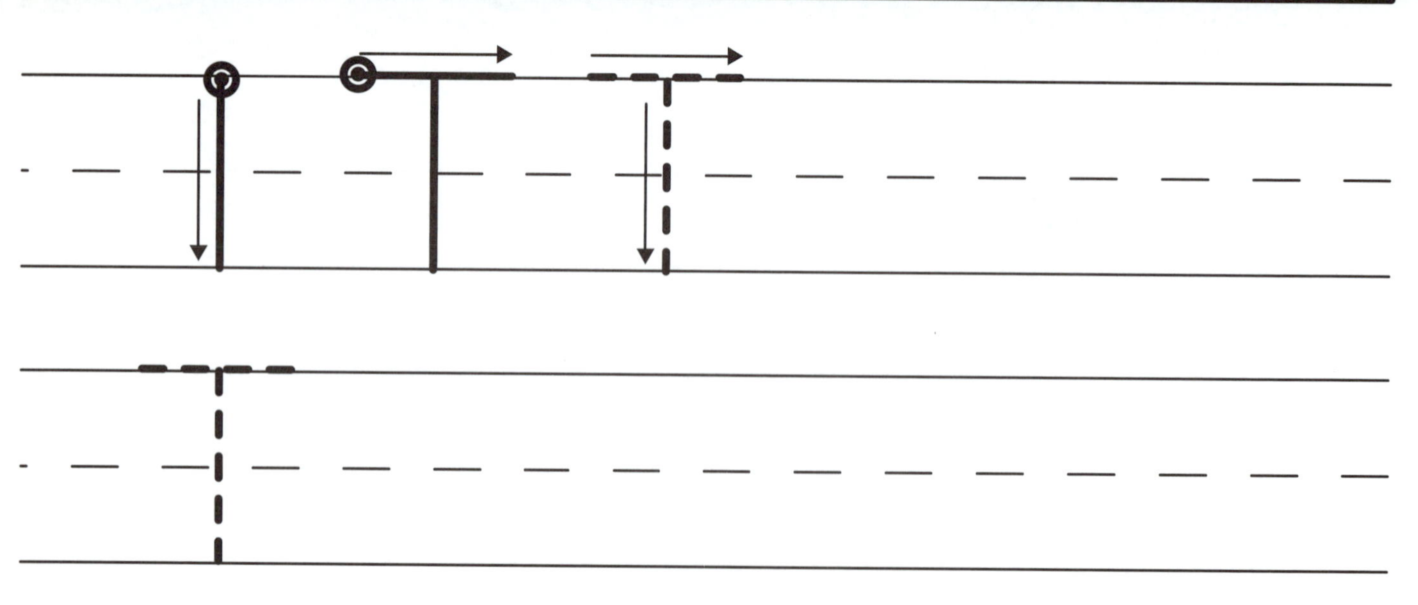

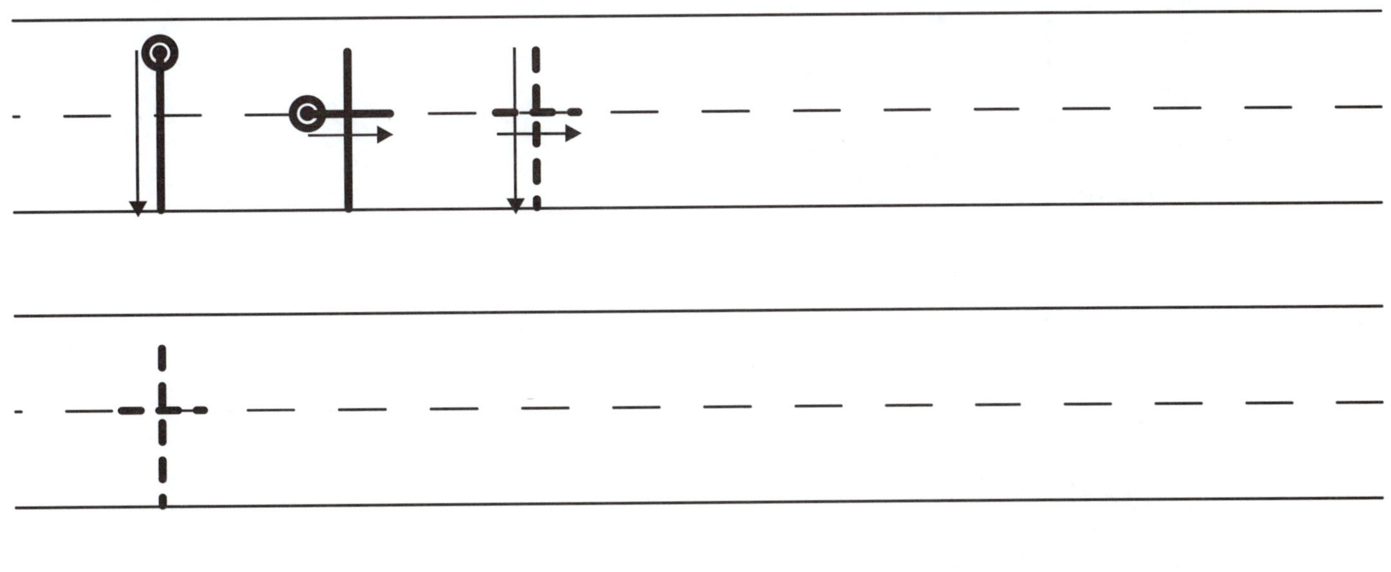

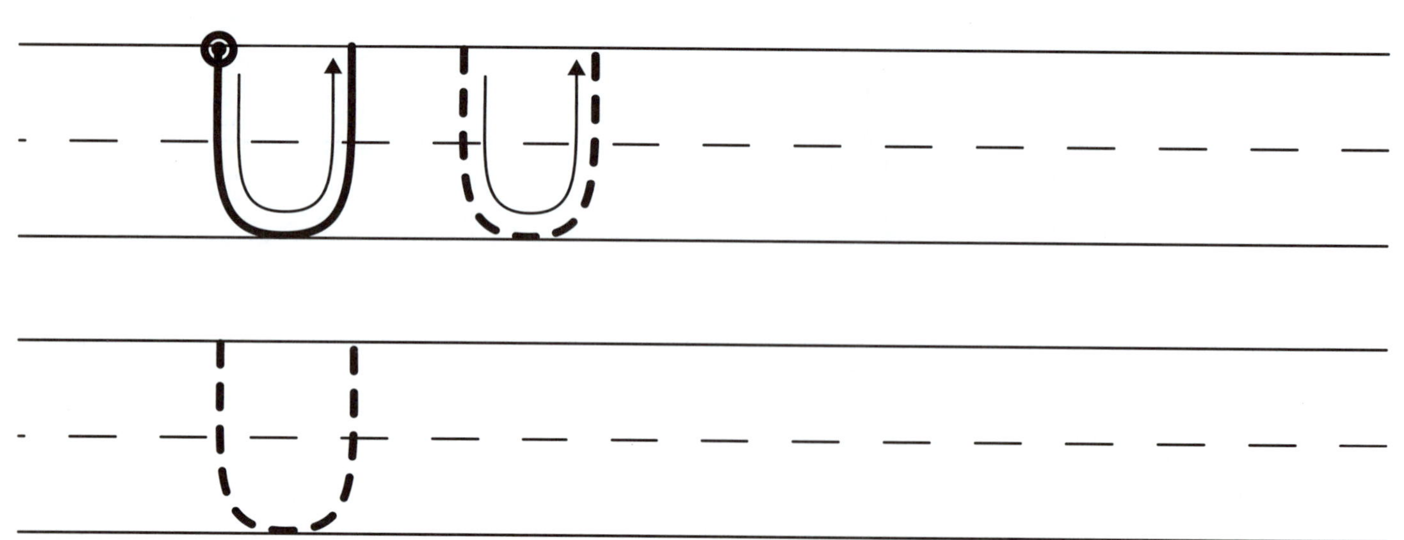

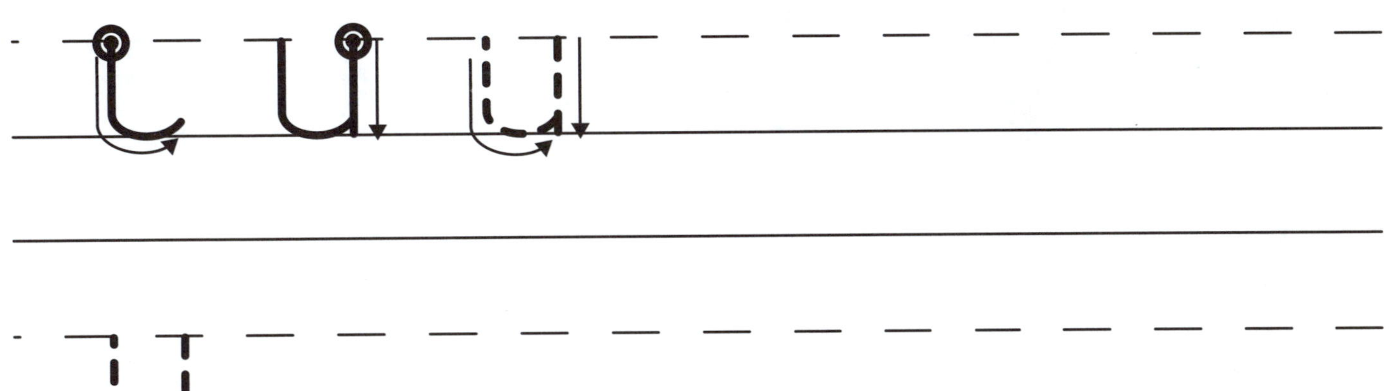
u u u
u

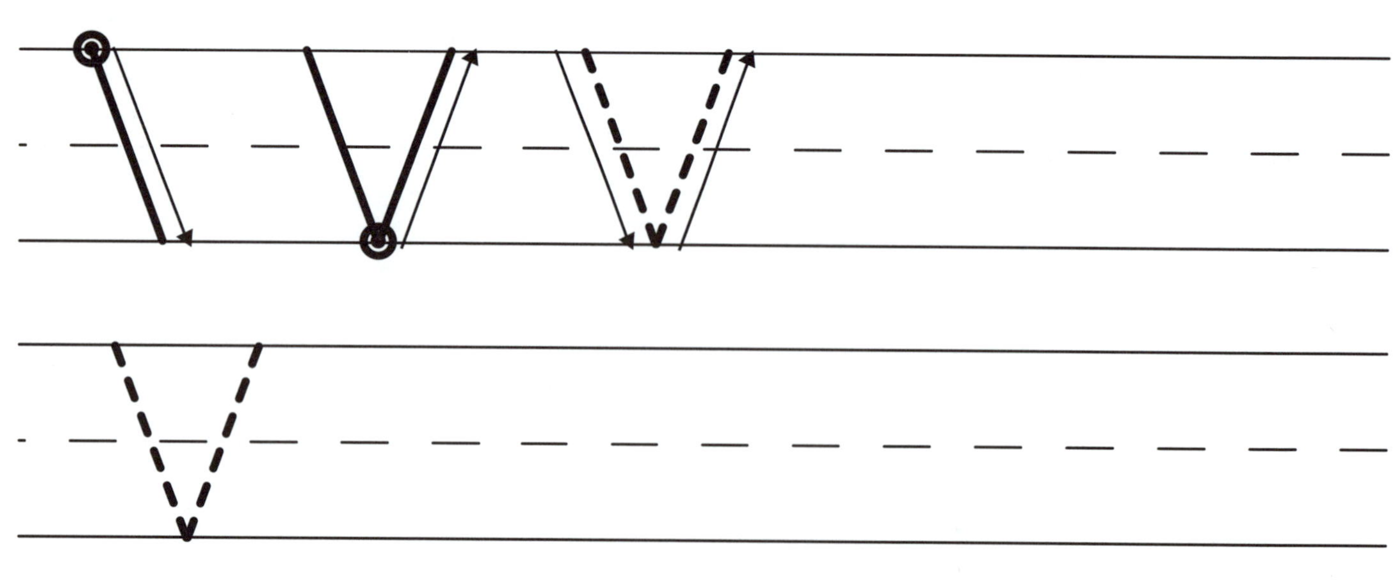

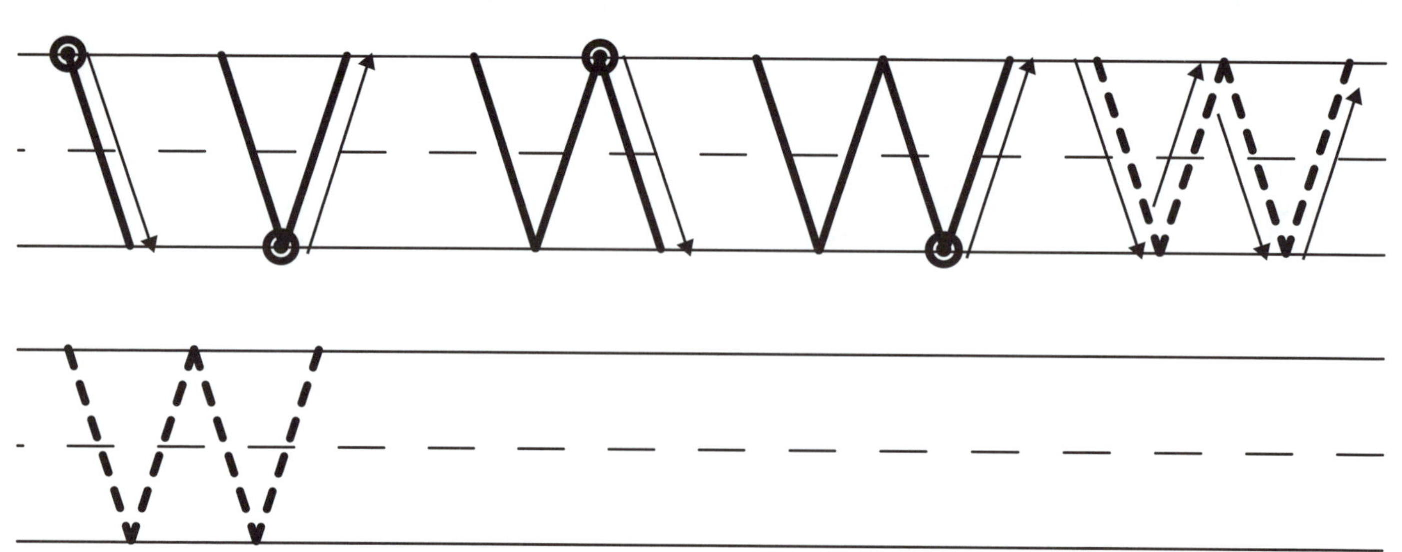

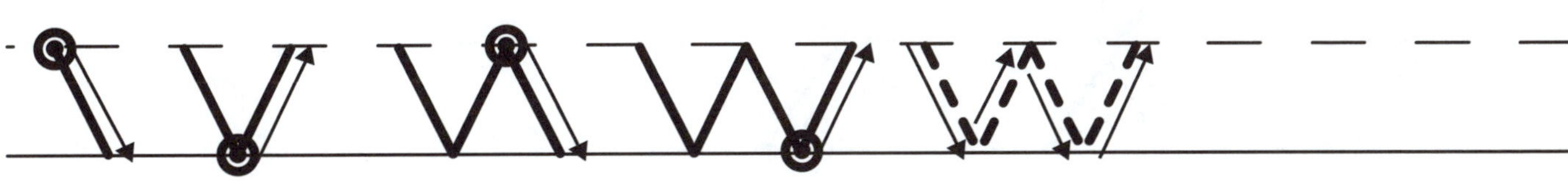

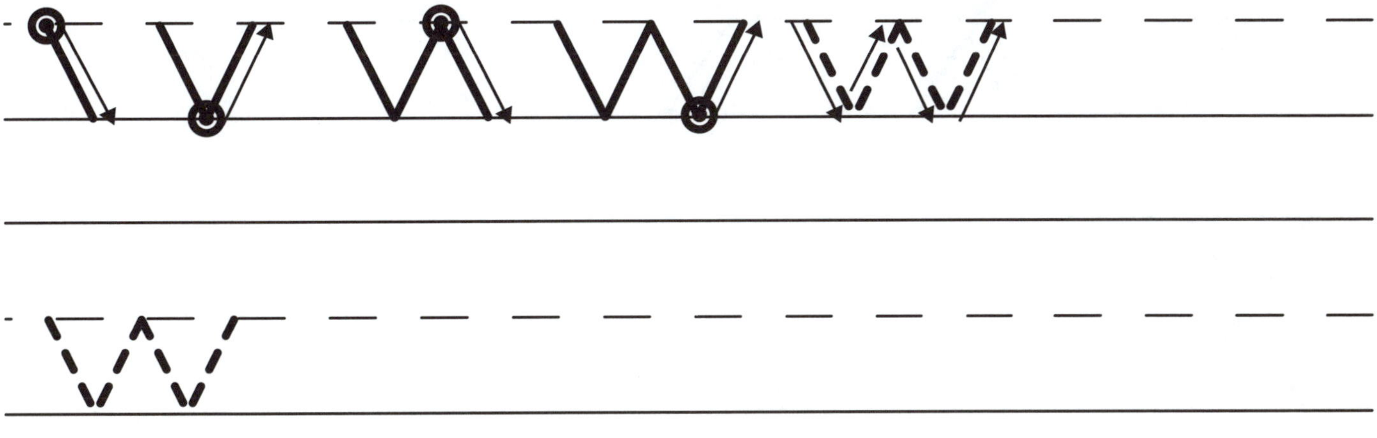

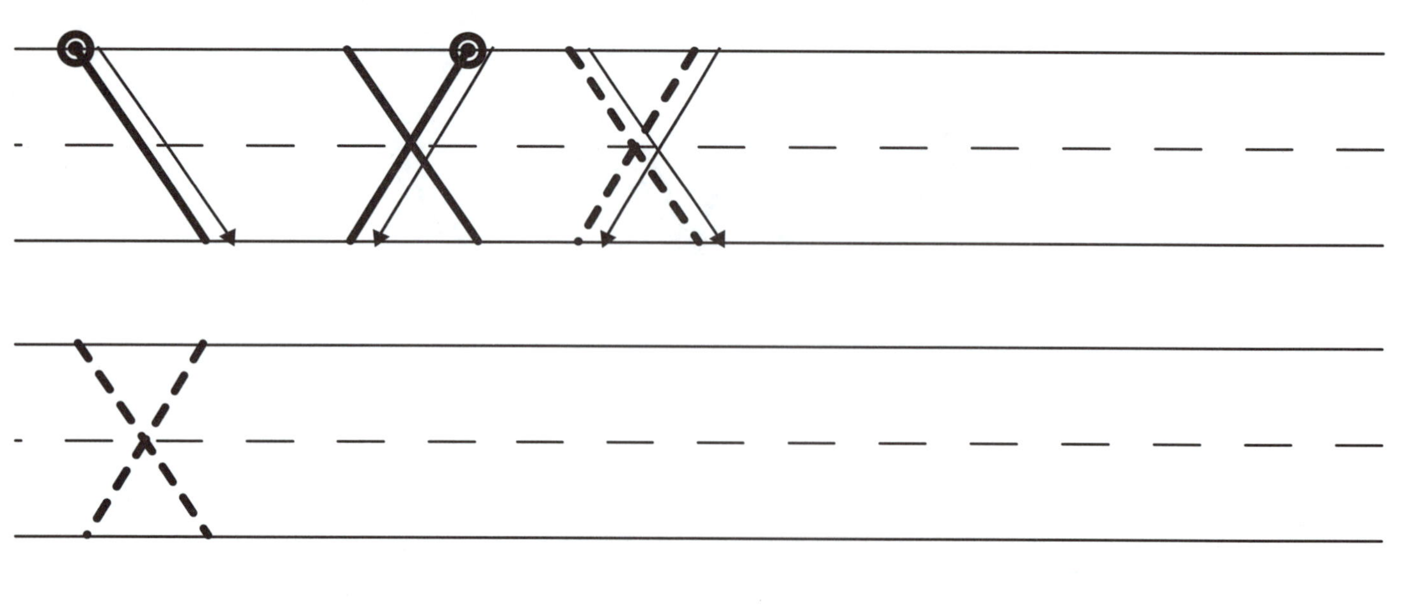

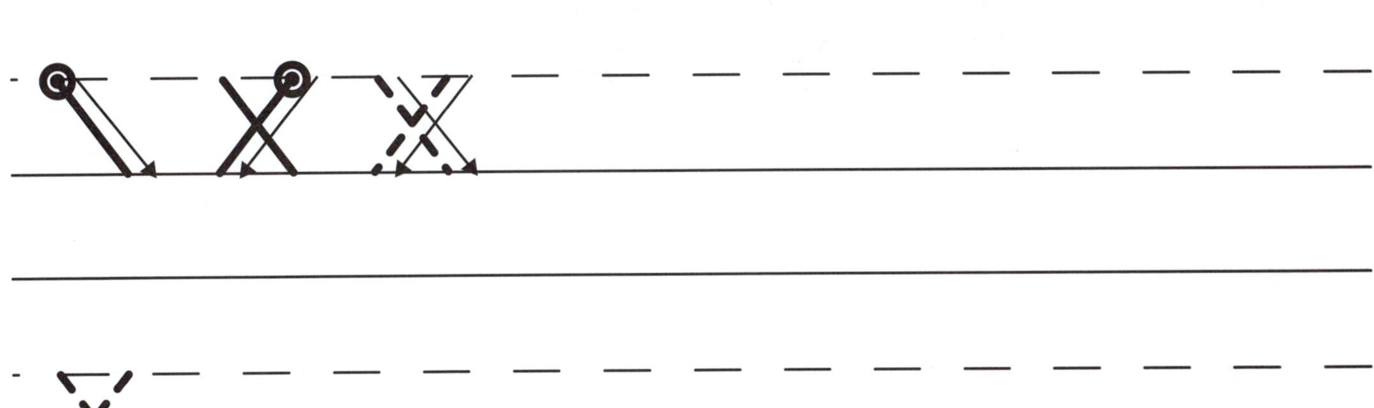

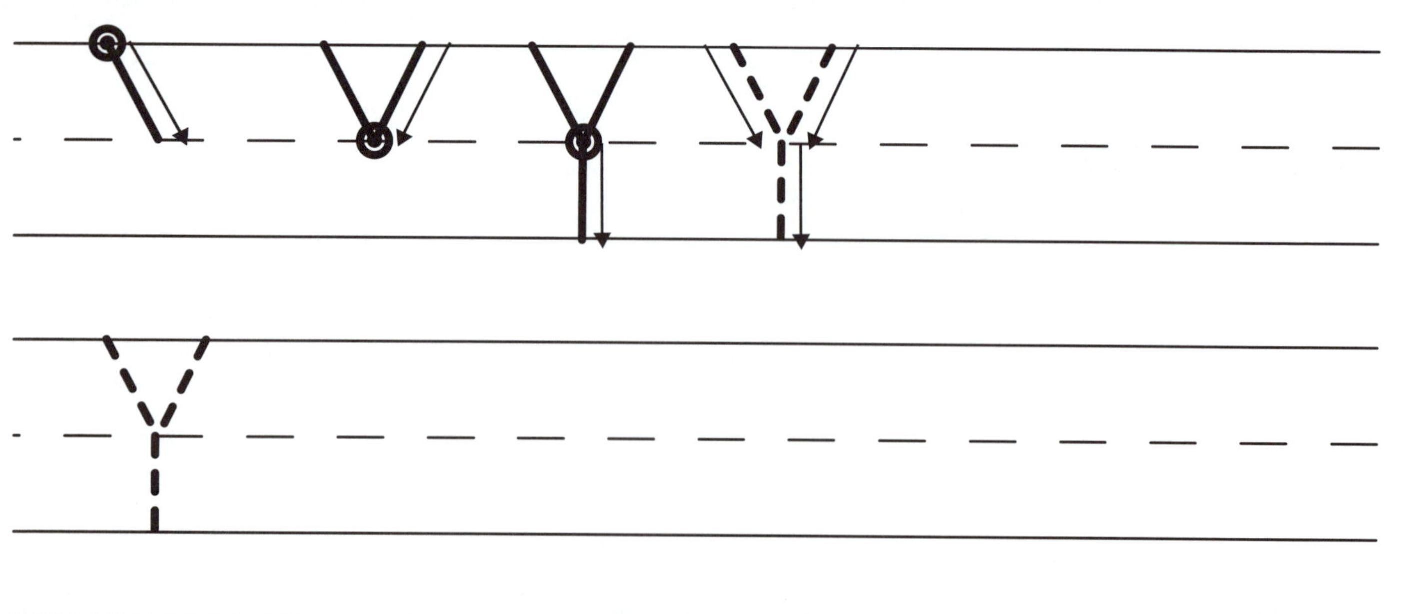

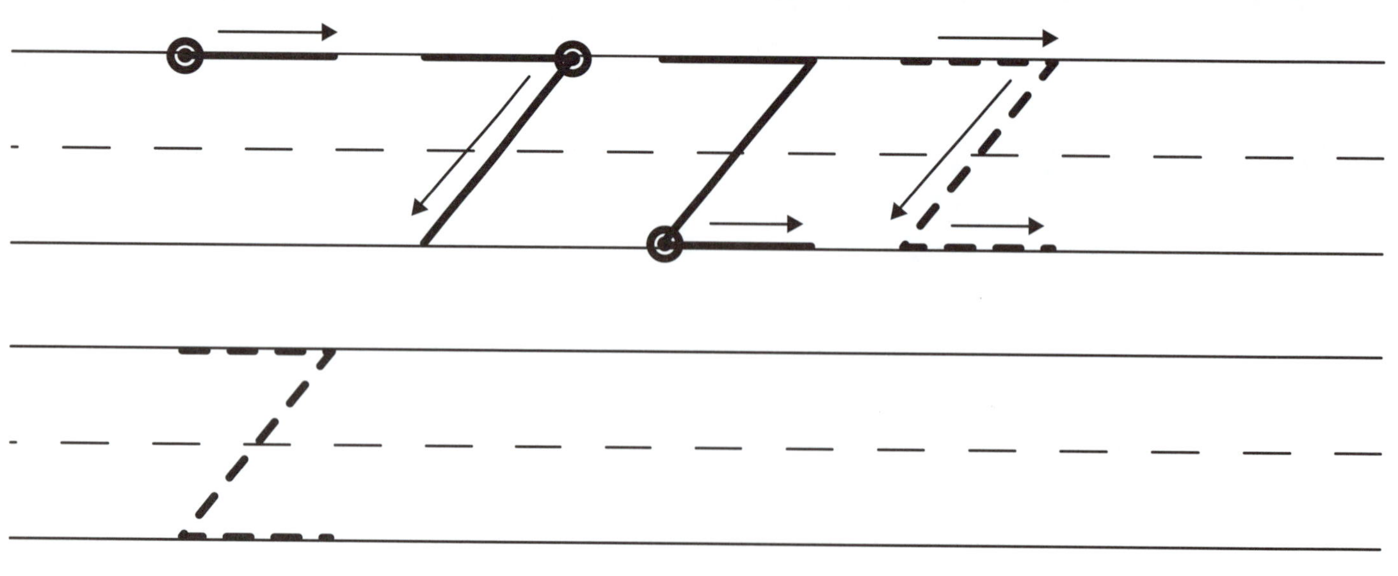

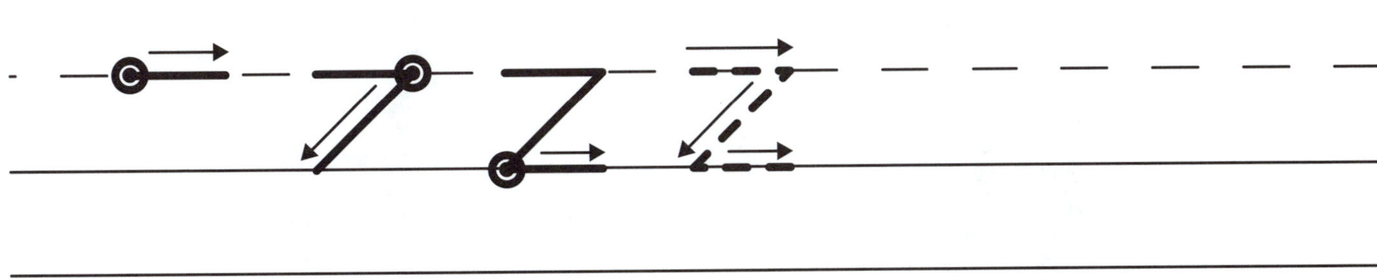

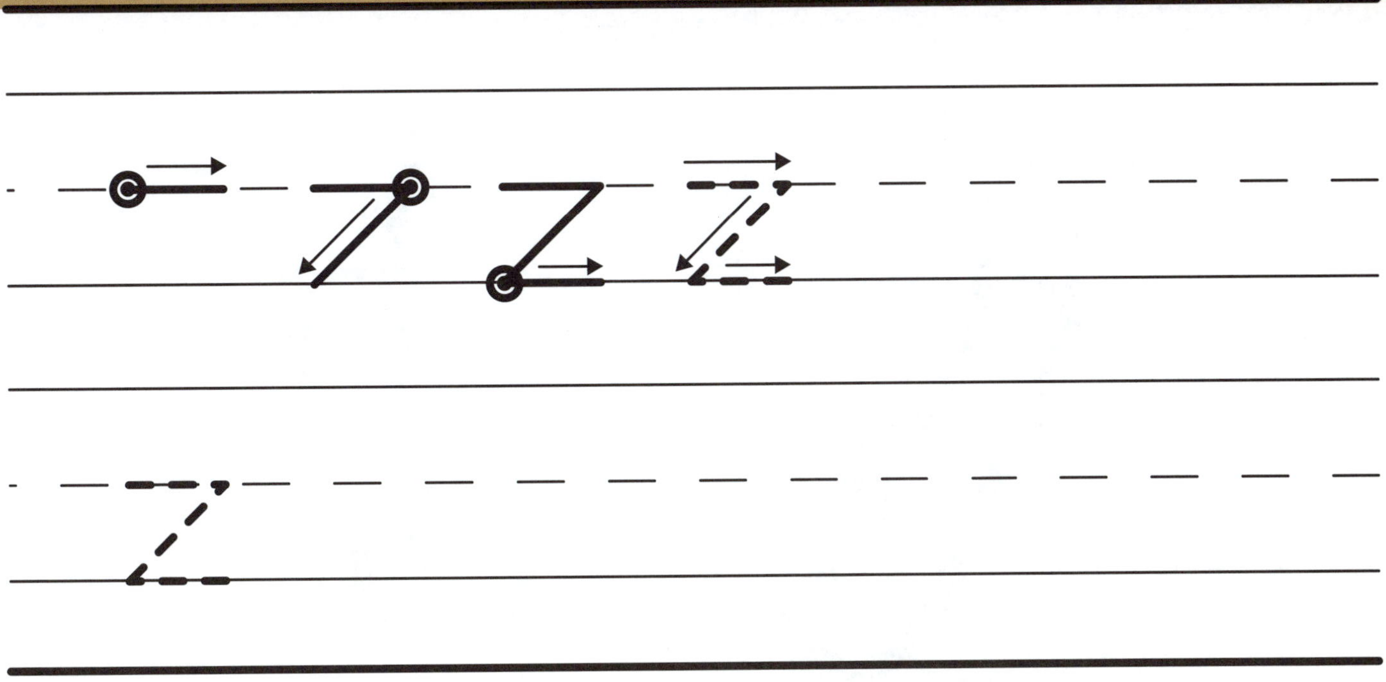

Connect the dots starting with 'A,' connect the dots starting with '1' and then color the picture.

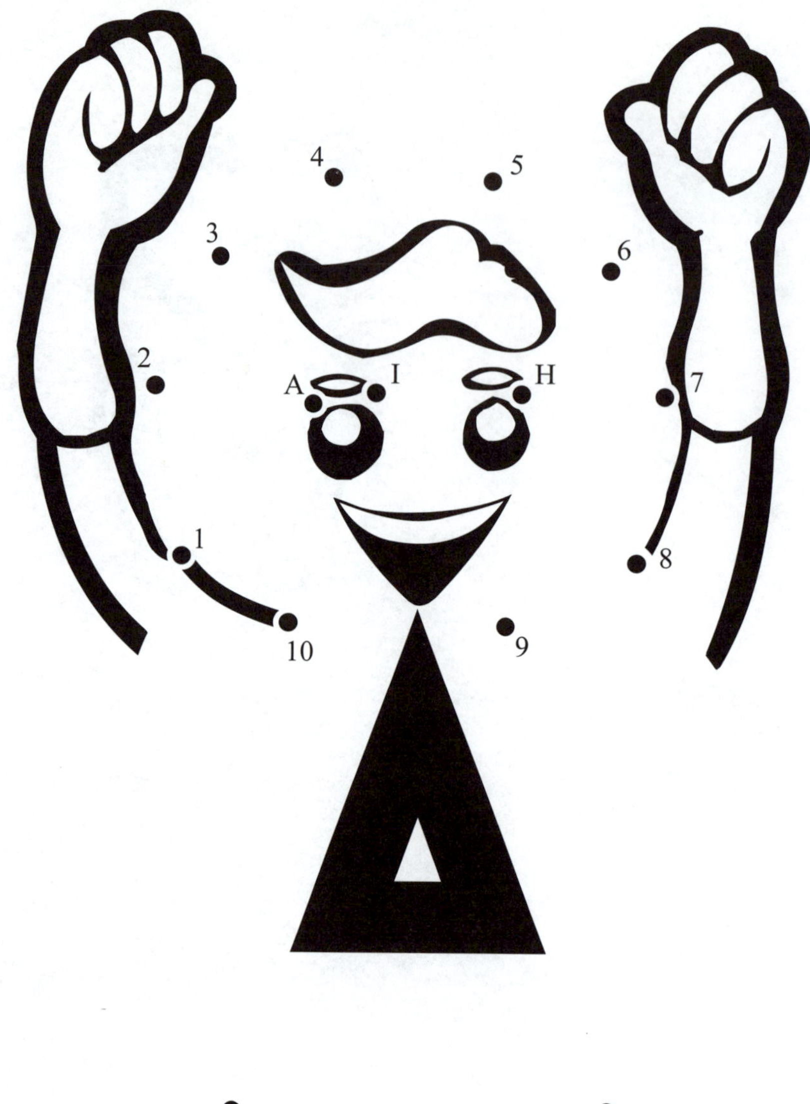

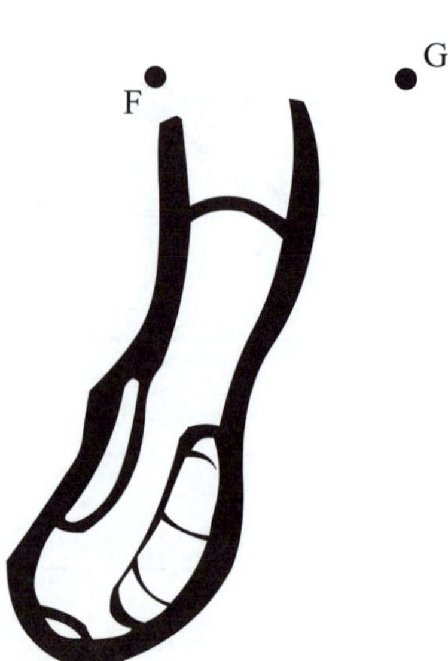

Connect the dots starting with 'A,' connect the dots starting with '1' and then color the picture.

Connect the dots starting with 'A,' connect the dots starting with '1' and then color the picture.

Connect the dots starting with 'A,' connect the dots starting with '1' and then color the picture.

Connect the dots starting with 'A,' connect the dots starting with '1' and then color the picture.

Connect the dots starting with 'A,' connect the dots starting with '1' and then color the picture.

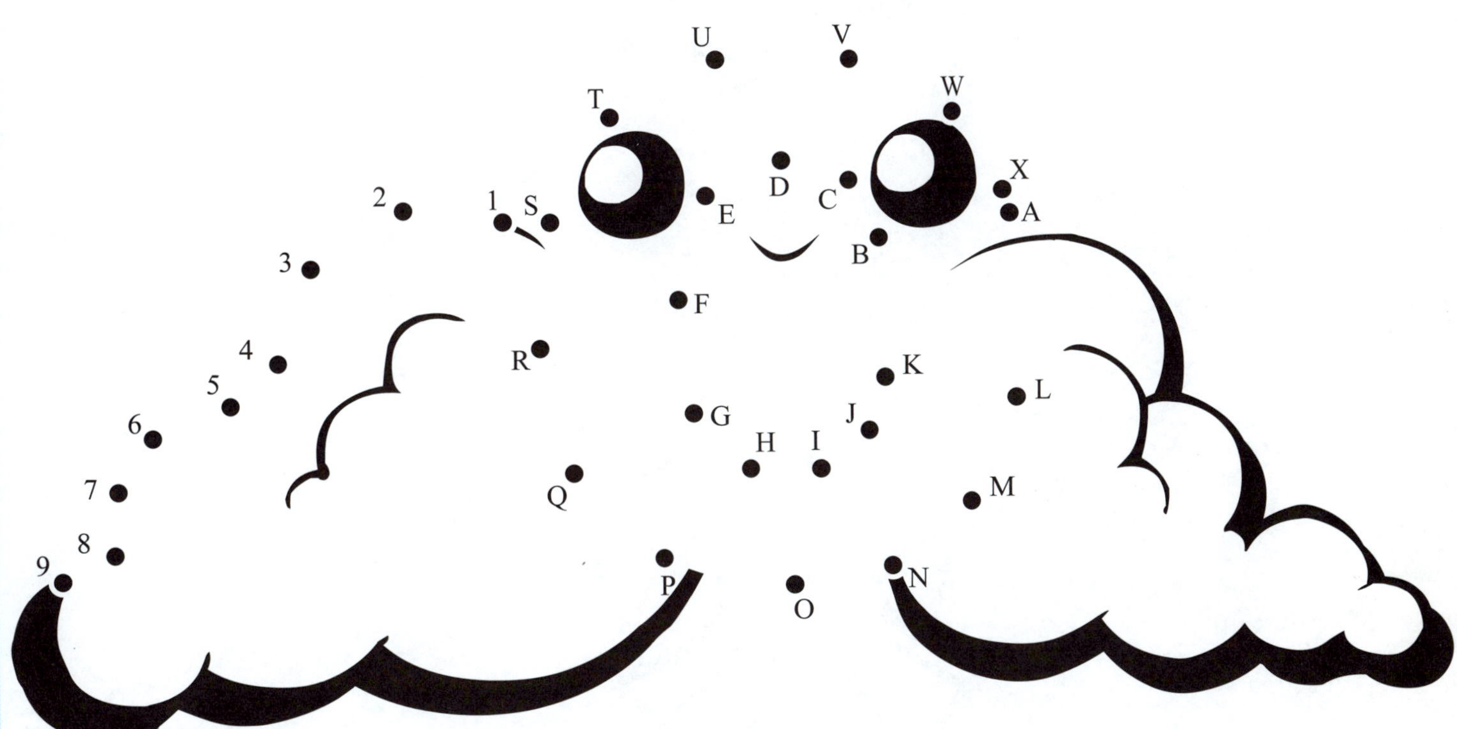

Connect the dots starting with 'A,' connect the dots starting with '1' and then color the picture.

Connect the dots starting with 'A,' connect the dots starting with '1' and then color the picture.

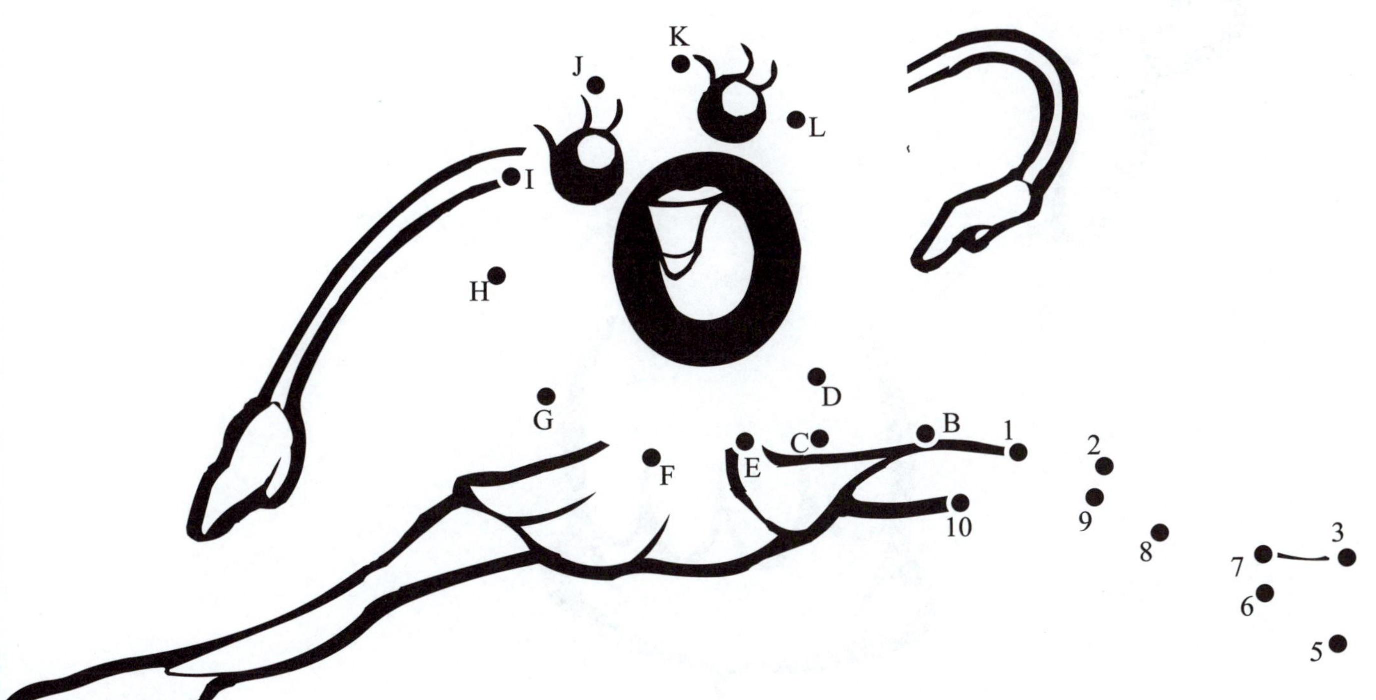

Connect the dots starting with 'A,' connect the dots starting with '1' and then color the picture.

Connect the dots starting with 'A,' connect the dots starting with '1' and then color the picture.

Connect the dots starting with 'A,' connect the dots starting with '1' and then color the picture.

Connect the dots starting with 'A,' connect the dots starting with '1' and then color the picture.

Connect the dots starting with 'A,' connect the dots starting with '1' and then color the picture.

Connect the dots starting with 'A,' connect the dots starting with '1' and then color the picture.

Connect the dots starting with 'A,' connect the dots starting with '1' and then color the picture.

Connect the dots starting with 'A,' connect the dots starting with '1' and then color the picture.

Connect the dots starting with 'A,' connect the dots starting with '1' and then color the picture.

Connect the dots starting with 'A,' connect the dots starting with '1' and then color the picture.

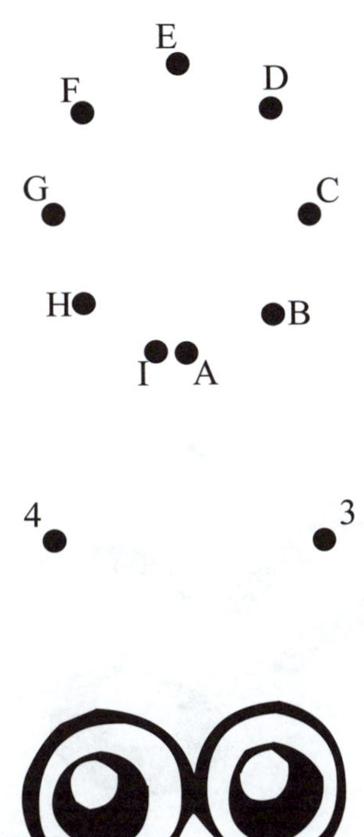

Connect the dots starting with 'A,' connect the dots starting with '1' and then color the picture.

Connect the dots starting with 'A,' connect the dots starting with '1' and then color the picture.

Connect the dots starting with 'A,' connect the dots starting with '1' and then color the picture.

Connect the dots starting with 'A,' connect the dots starting with '1' and then color the picture.

K J H G I F C B A N 4 2 1 5 3 6 L M D E

Connect the dots starting with 'A,' connect the dots starting with '1' and then color the picture.

Connect the dots starting with 'A,' connect the dots starting with '1' and then color the picture.

Connect the dots starting with 'A,' connect the dots starting with '1' and then color the picture.

Connect the dots starting with 'A,' connect the dots starting with '1' and then color the picture.

Connect the dots starting with 'A,' connect the dots starting with '1' and then color the picture.

Connect the dots starting with 'A,' connect the dots starting with '1' and then color the picture.

Connect the dots starting with 'A,' connect the dots starting with '1' and then color the picture.

Connect the dots starting with 'A,' connect the dots starting with '1' and then color the picture.

Connect the dots starting with 'A,' connect the dots starting with '1' and then color the picture.

Connect the dots starting with 'A,' connect the dots starting with '1' and then color the picture.

Connect the dots starting with 'A,' connect the dots starting with '1' and then color the picture.

Connect the dots starting with 'A,' connect the dots starting with '1' and then color the picture.

Connect the dots starting with 'A,' connect the dots starting with '1' and then color the picture.

Connect the dots starting with 'A,' connect the dots starting with '1' and then color the picture.

Connect the dots starting with 'A,' connect the dots starting with '1' and then color the picture.

Connect the dots starting with 'A,' connect the dots starting with '1' and then color the picture.

Connect the dots starting with 'A,' connect the dots starting with '1' and then color the picture.

Connect the dots starting with 'A,' connect the dots starting with '1' and then color the picture.

Connect the dots starting with 'A,' connect the dots starting with '1' and then color the picture.

Connect the dots starting with 'A,' connect the dots starting with '1' and then color the picture.

Connect the dots starting with 'A,' connect the dots starting with '1' and then color the picture.

B

2 3

Connect the dots starting with 'A,' connect the dots starting with '1' and then color the picture.

Connect the dots starting with 'A,' connect the dots starting with '1' and then color the picture.

Connect the dots starting with 'A,' connect the dots starting with '1' and then color the picture.

Connect the dots starting with 'A,' connect the dots starting with '1' and then color the picture.

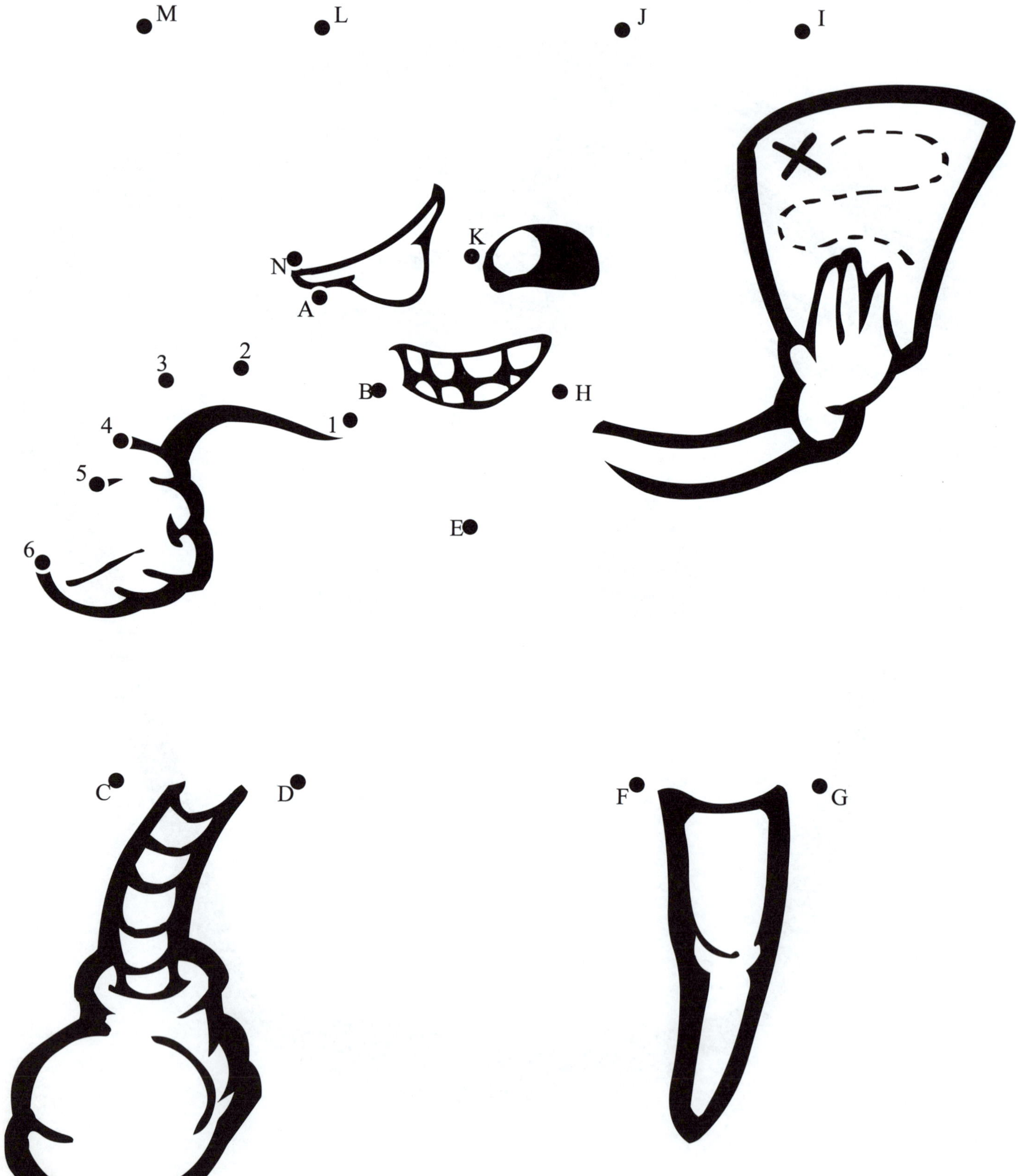

M L J I

K
N
A

3 2
B H
4 1

5

E
6

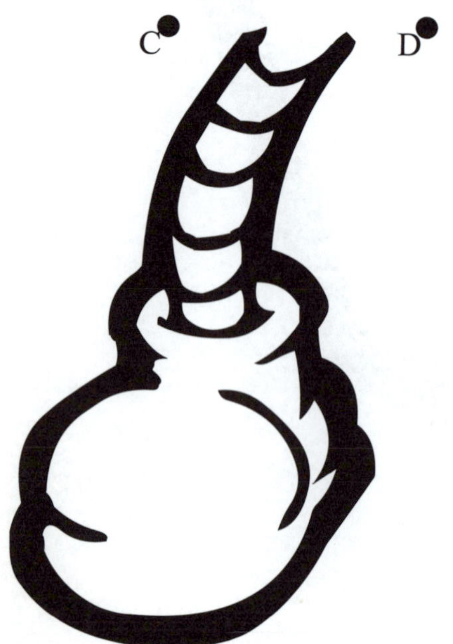

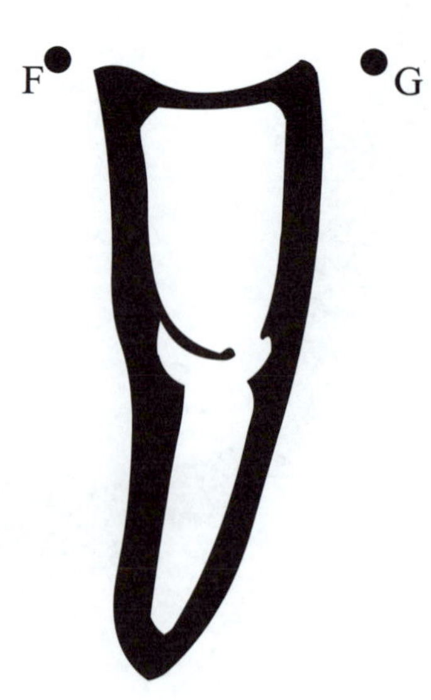

C D F G

Connect the dots starting with 'A,' connect the dots starting with '1' and then color the picture.

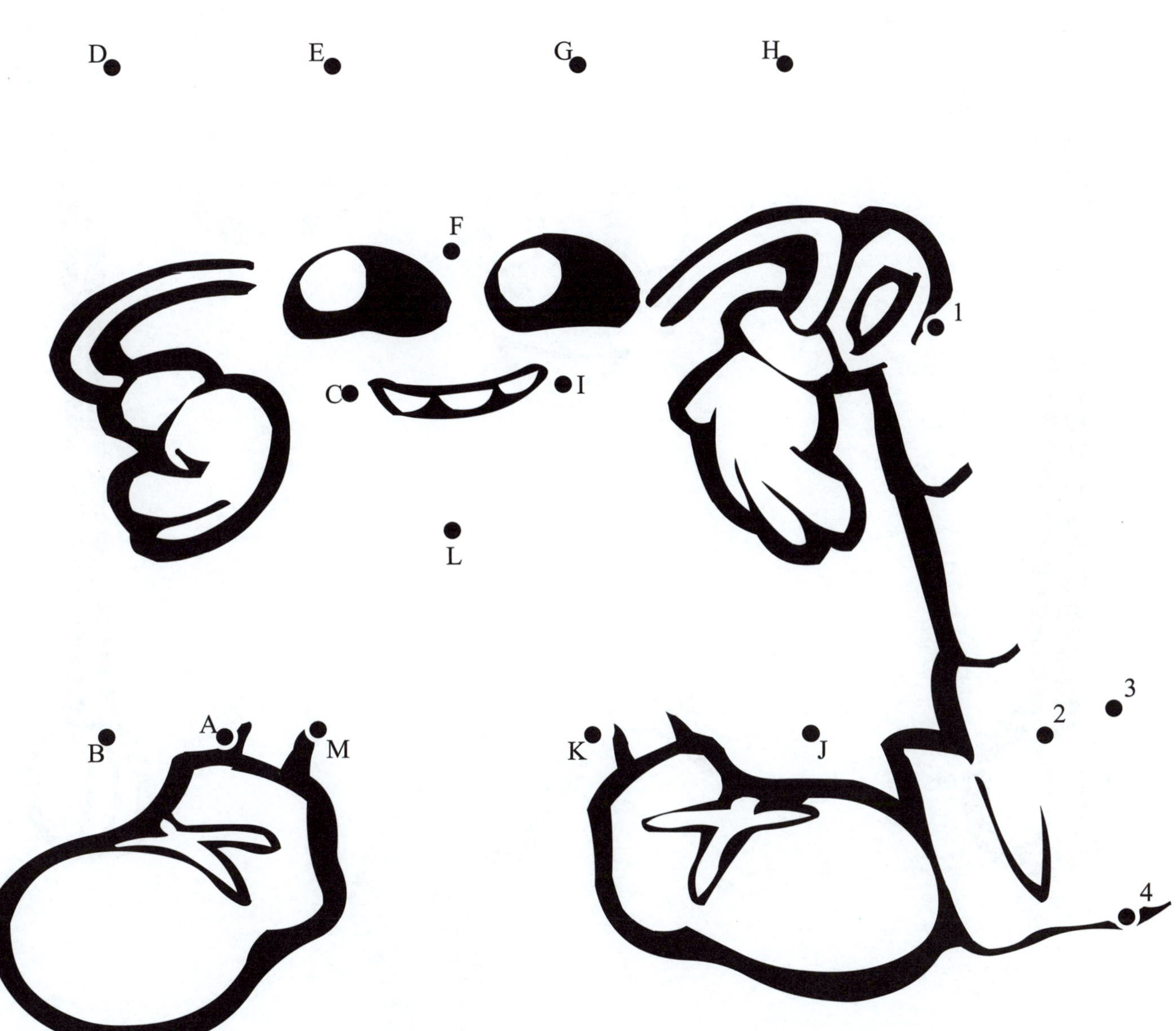

Connect the dots starting with 'A,' connect the dots starting with '1' and then color the picture.

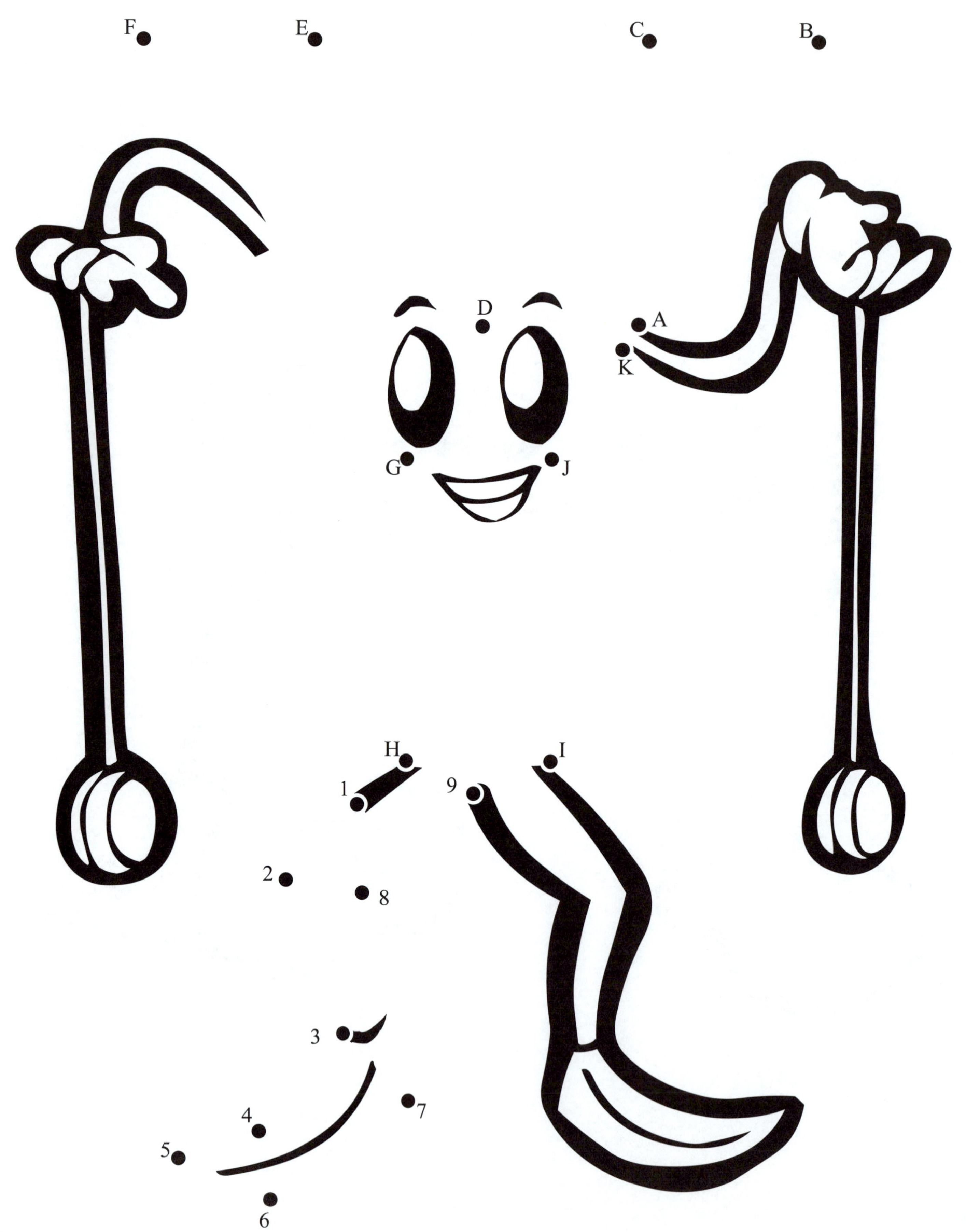

Connect the dots starting with 'A,' connect the dots starting with '1' and then color the picture.

Connect the dots starting with 'A,' connect the dots starting with '1' and then color the picture.

Connect the dots starting with 'A,' connect the dots starting with '1' and then color the picture.

Circle the letters.

a

5

7

e

r

y

q

9

p

Circle the letters.

z

3

g

m

y

v

r

9

10

Draw a line from the uppercase letter to the lowercase letter.

A g

G l

B a

L b

M m

Draw a line from the uppercase letter to the lowercase letter.

D r

Y k

K y

T d

R t

Draw a line from the uppercase letter to the lowercase letter.

F i

W o

N n

O f

I w

Draw a line from the uppercase letter to the lowercase letter.

J p

S e

P j

E q

Q s

Draw a line from the uppercase letter to the lowercase letter.

H

v

C

c

U

h

Z

u

V

z

Draw a line from the uppercase letter to the lowercase letter.

X	k
T	d
O	o
D	t
K	x

Circle the 5 things that are different in the 2 pictures.

Circle the 5 things that are different in the 2 pictures.

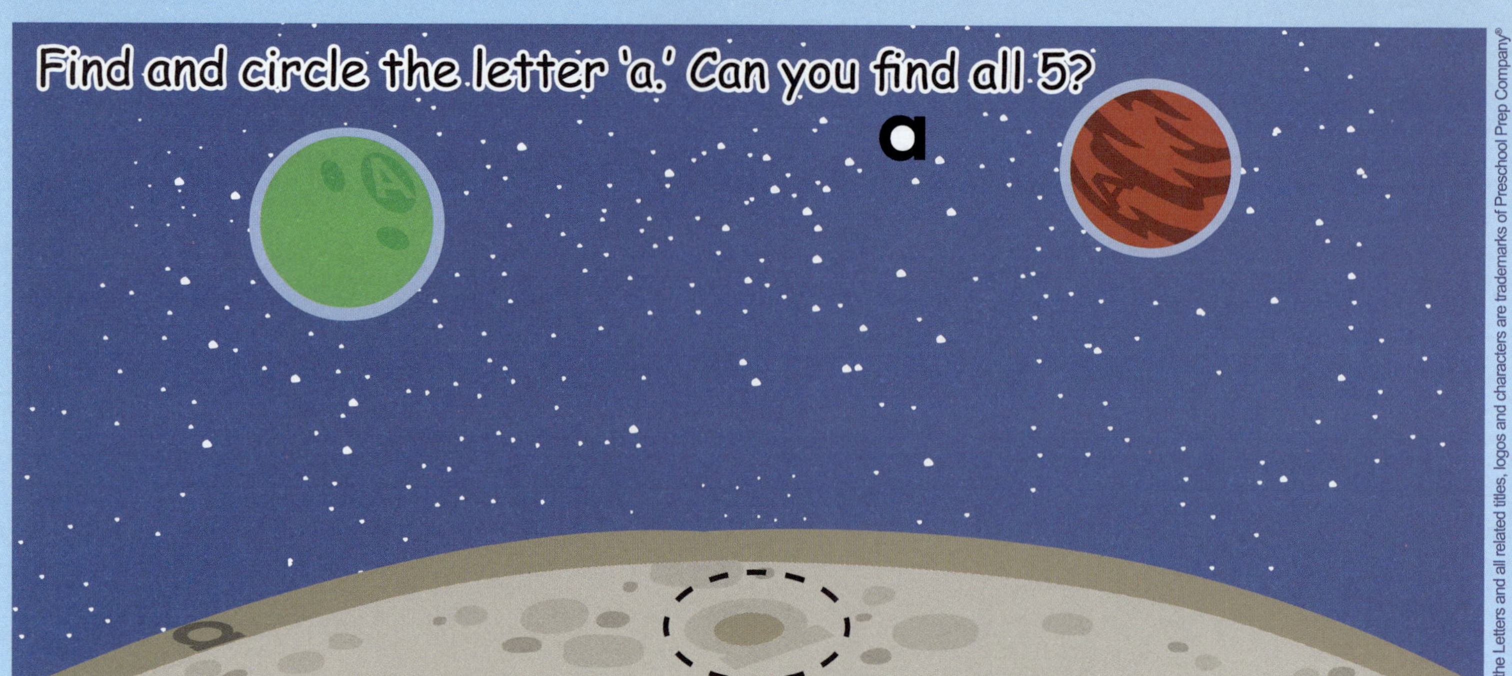

Write the missing upper or lowercase letter.

__a

__a A__

Circle the apples that have the letter 'a' inside.

Draw a line while connecting the 'a' letters to find your way across the maze!

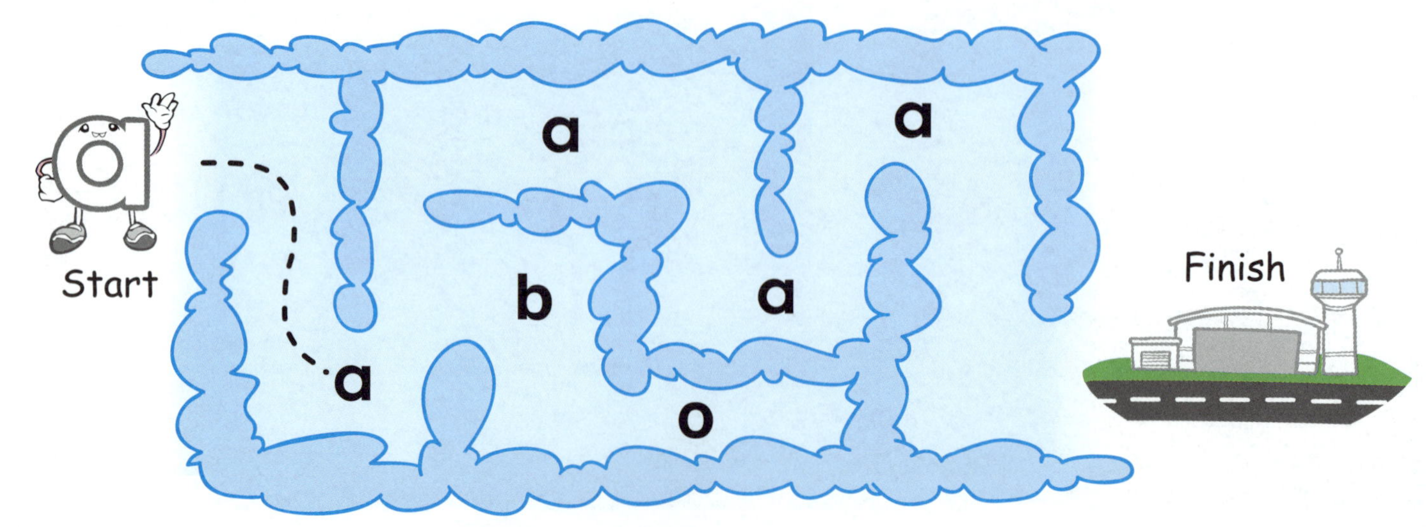

Find and circle the letter 'b.' Can you find all 5?

Circle the matching letters in each row.

Connect the lowercase 'b' letters to the uppercase 'B.'

b a b b B b b p b b d b

Complete the pattern below:

Find and circle the letter 'c.' Can you find all 5?

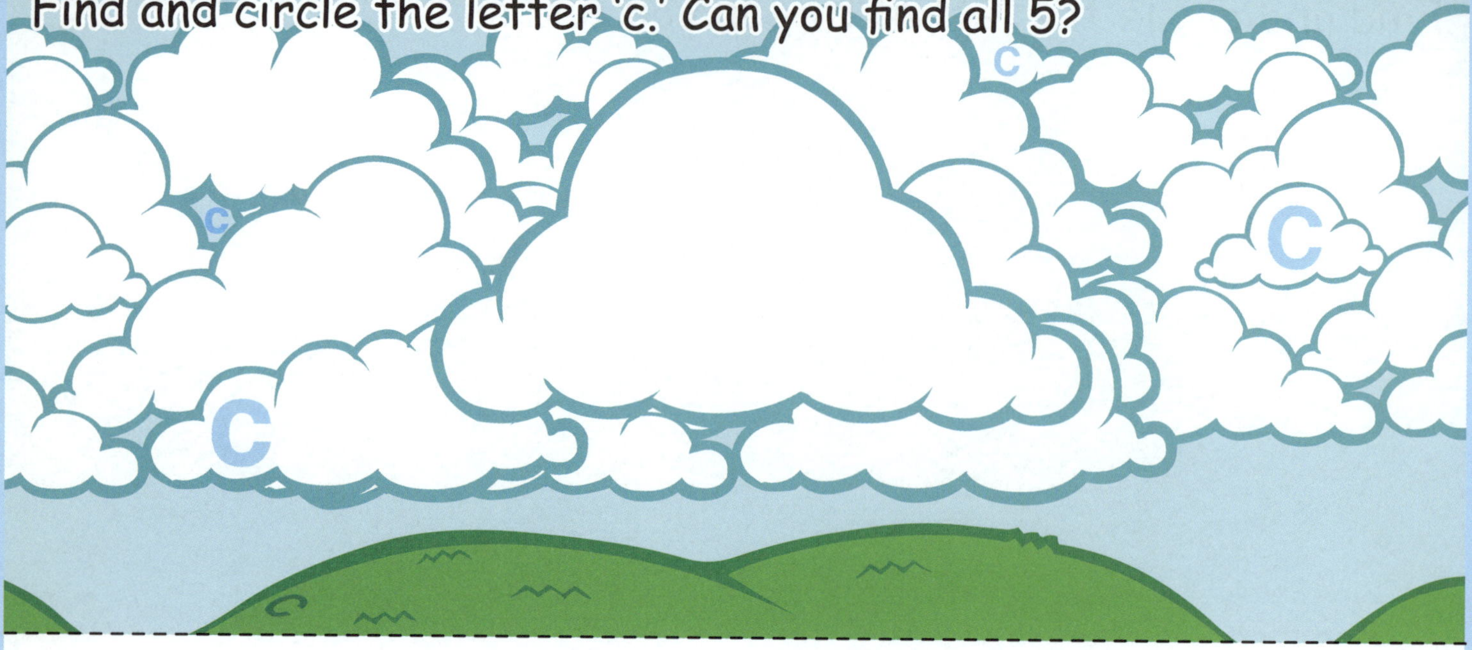
c
c
c
c
c

Draw a line to match the uppercase & lowercase letters.

A	B
b	c
C	a

Fill in the missing 'c' letters.

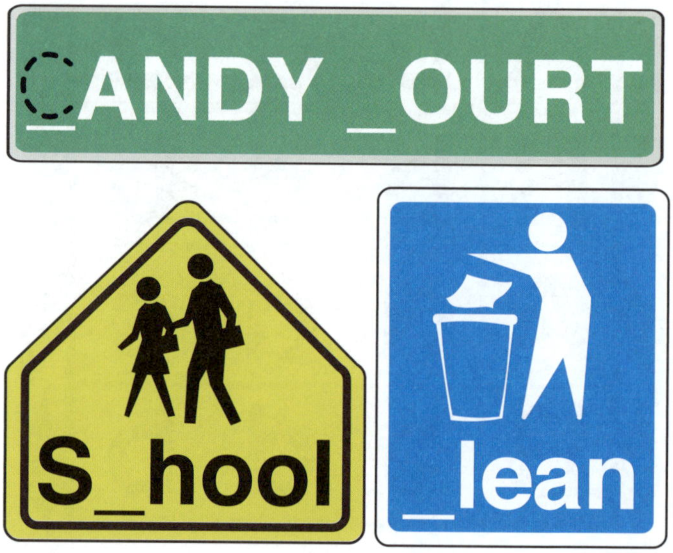
_ANDY _OURT
S_hool
_lean

Color the picture.

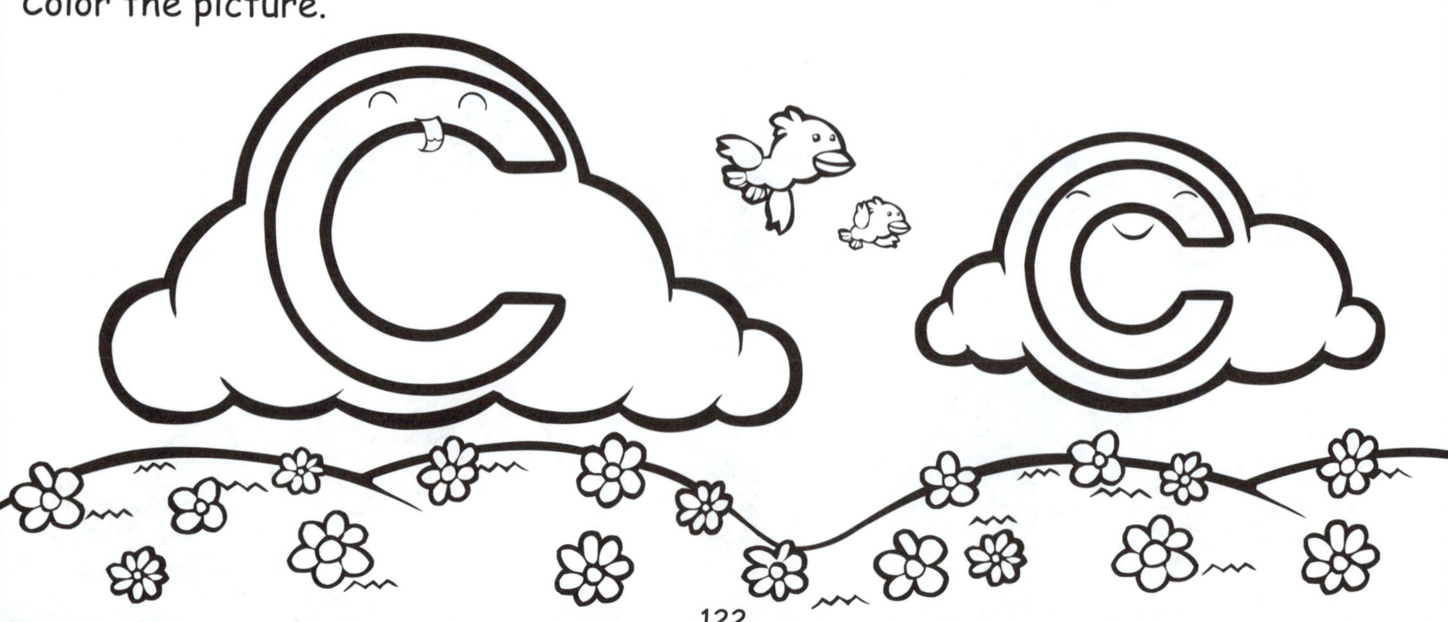

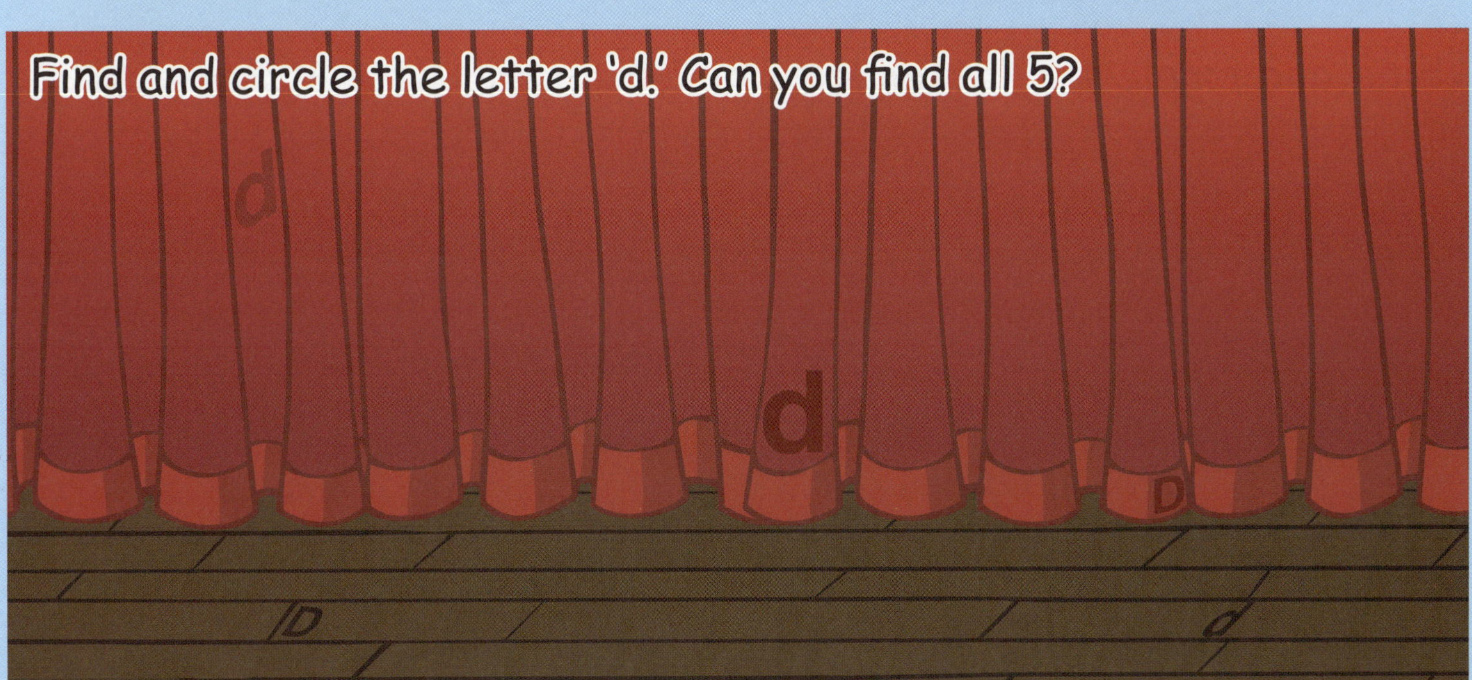

Write the missing upper or lowercase letter.

Circle the ducks that have the letter 'd' inside.

Draw a line while connecting the 'd' letters to find your way across the maze!

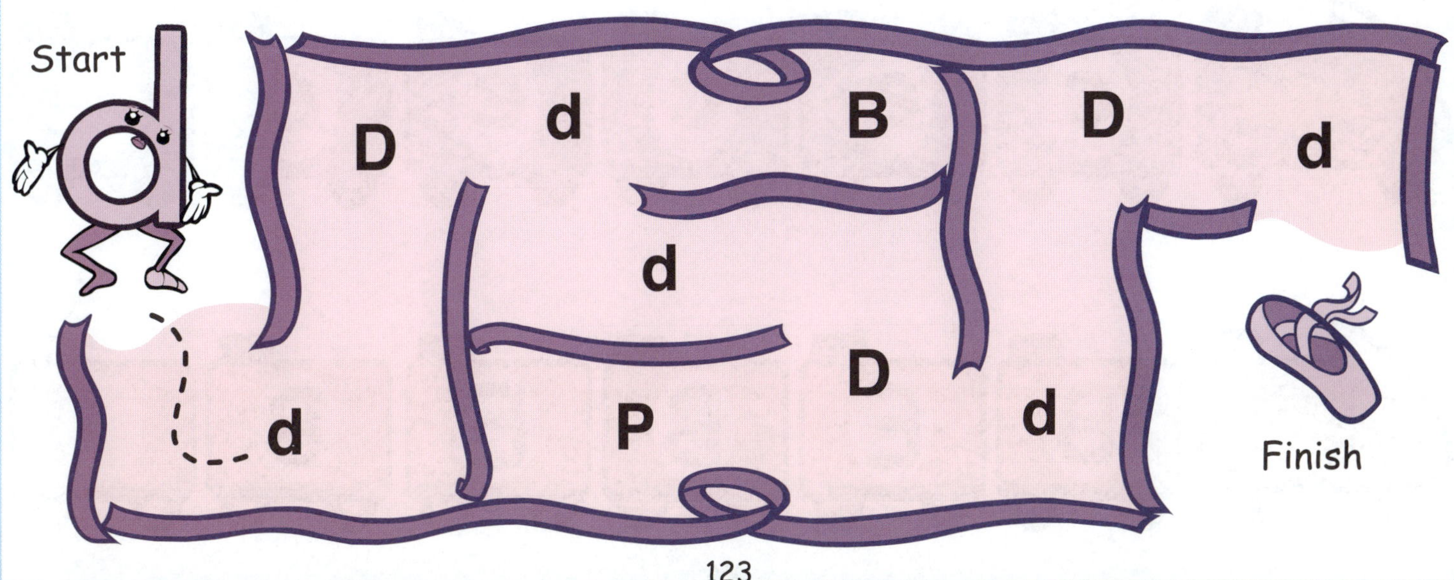

Find and circle the letter 'e.' Can you find all 5?

Circle the matching letters in each row.

Connect the lowercase 'e' letters to the uppercase 'E.'

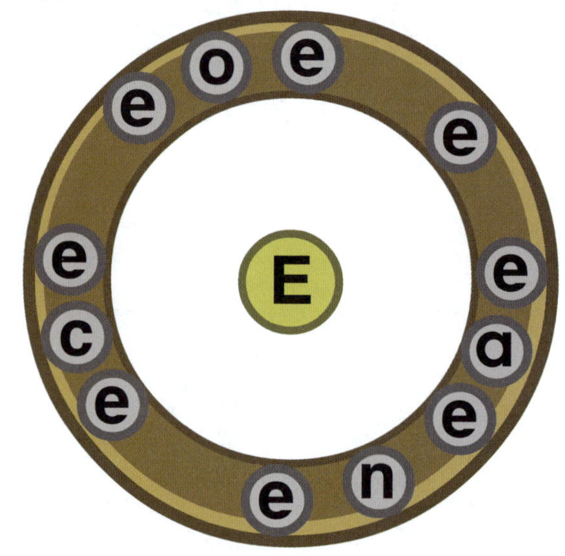

Complete the patterns below:

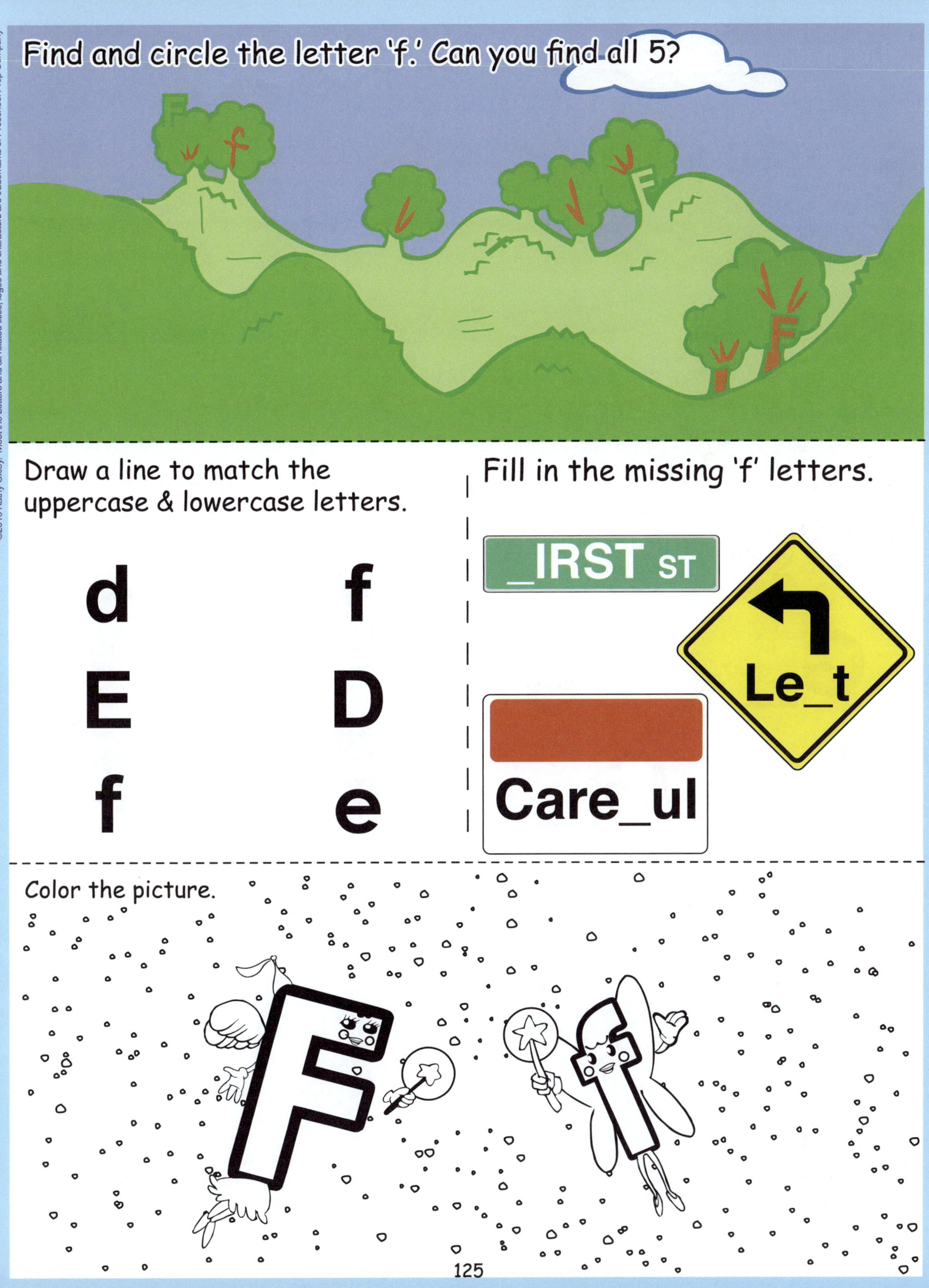
Find and circle the letter 'f.' Can you find all 5?
Draw a line to match the uppercase & lowercase letters.
d
f
E
D
f
e
Fill in the missing 'f' letters.
_IRST ST
Le_t
Care_ul
Color the picture.
125

Write the missing upper or lowercase letter.

G__ __g

__g G__

Circle the grapes that have the letter 'g' inside.

Draw a line while connecting the 'g' letters to find your way across the maze!

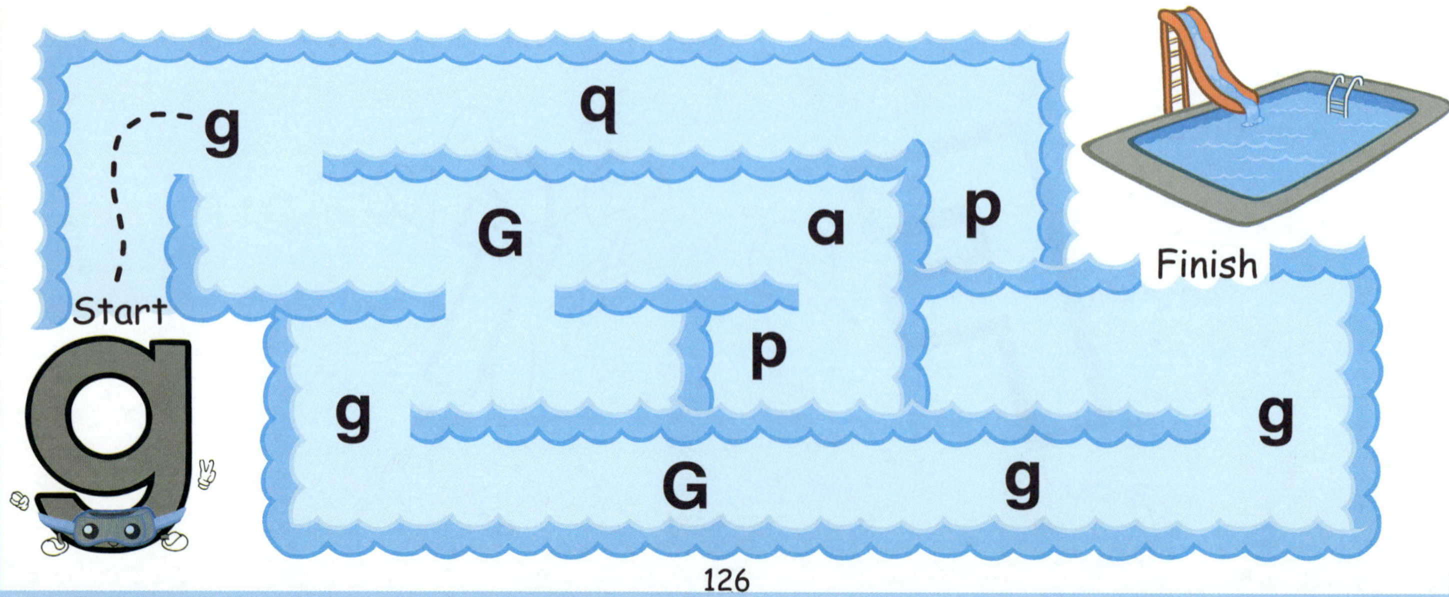

Find and circle the letter 'h.' Can you find all 5?

Circle the matching letters in each row.

Connect the lowercase 'h' letters to the uppercase 'H.'

Complete the patterns below:

Find and circle the letter 'i.' Can you find all 5?

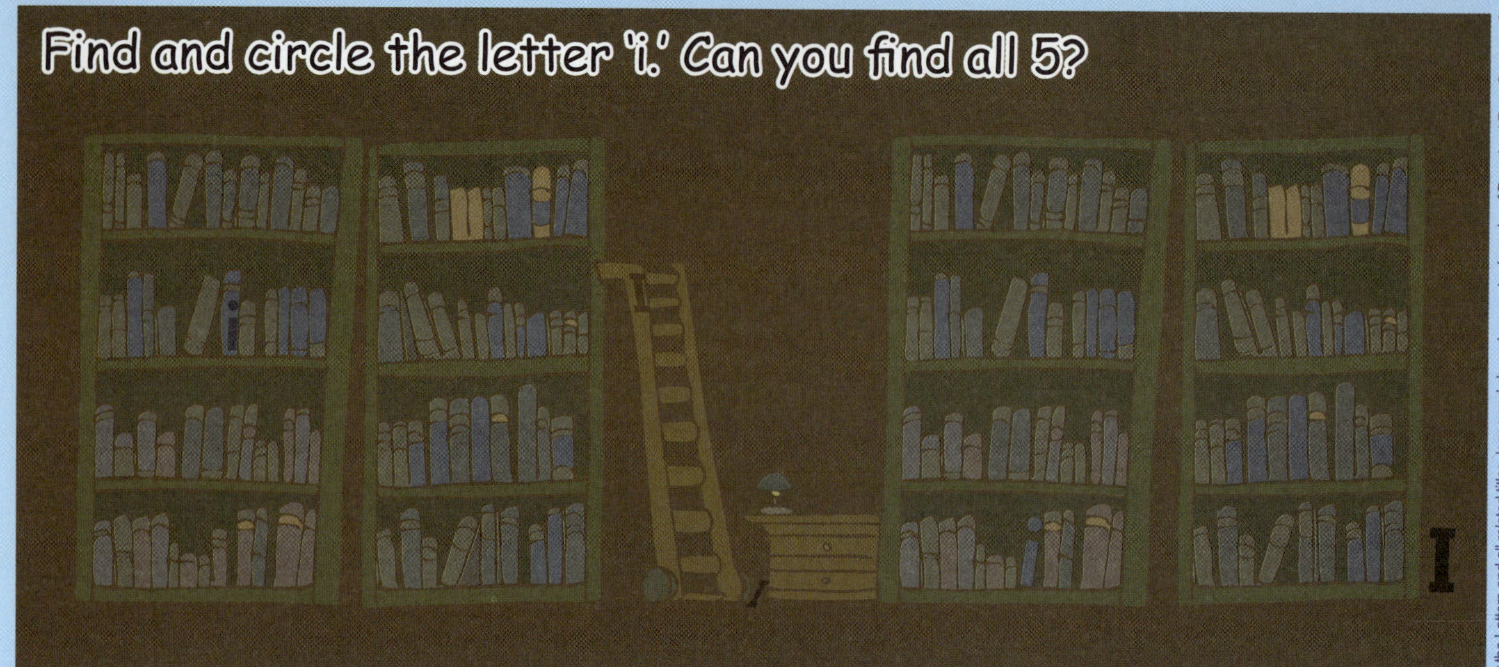

Draw a line to match the uppercase & lowercase letters.

G h

H I

i g

Fill in the missing 'i' letters.

Color the picture.

Find and circle the letter 'j.' Can you find all 5?

Write the missing upper or lowercase letter.

J___ ___j

___j J___

Circle the jars that have the letter 'j' inside.

i j C

j t j

Draw a line while connecting the 'j' letters to find your way across the maze!

Find and circle the letter 'k.' Can you find all 5?

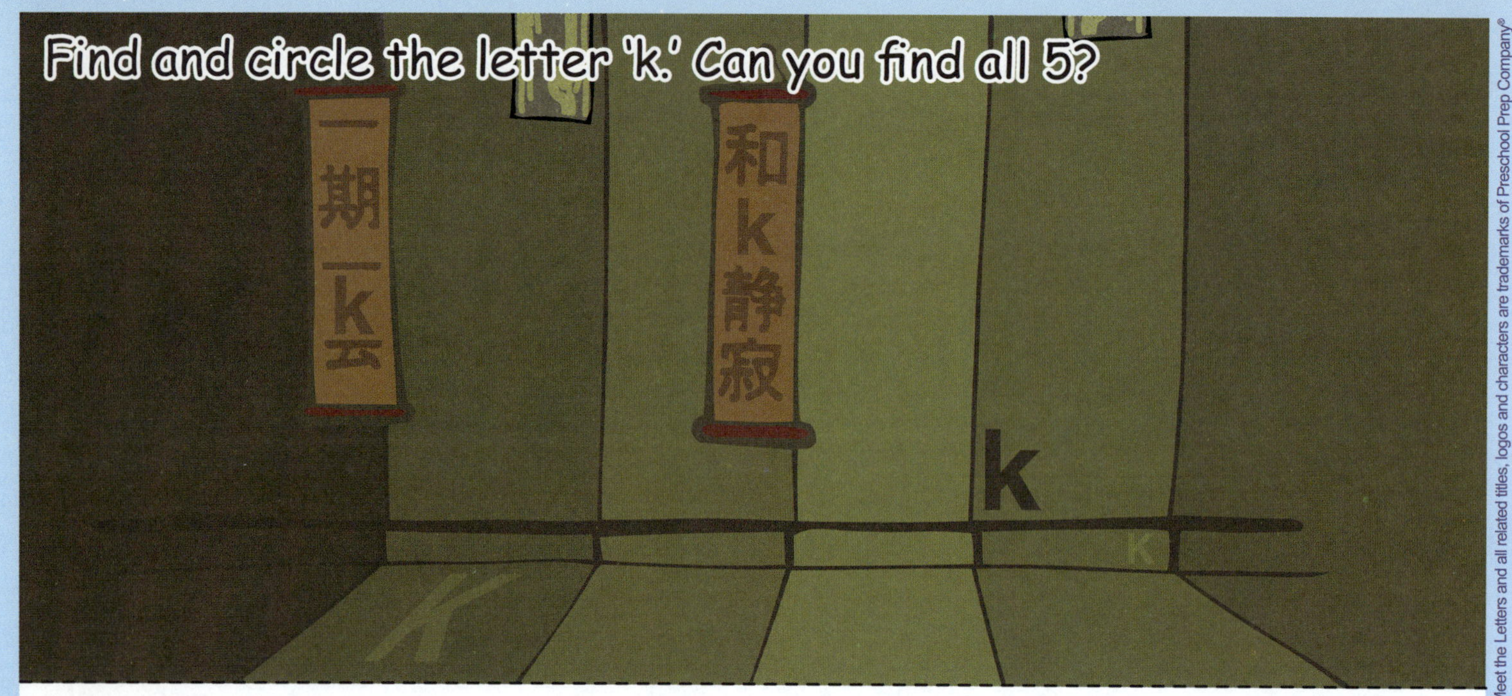

Circle the matching letters in each row.

Connect the lowercase 'k' letters to the uppercase 'K.'

Complete the patterns below:

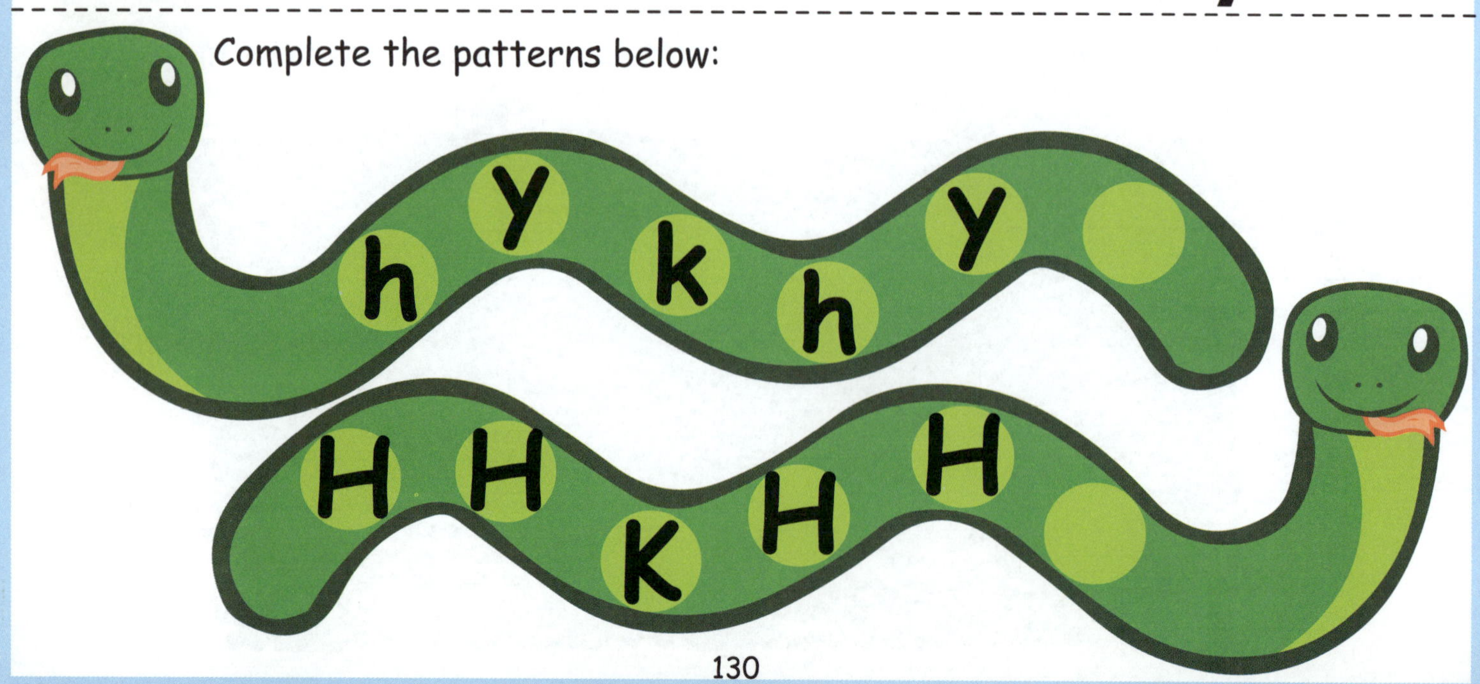

Find and circle the letter 'l.' Can you find all 5?
Draw a line to match the uppercase & lowercase letters.
j
k
K
l
L
J
Fill in the missing 'l' letters.
S_OW
CHI_DREN
YIE_D
_ITT_E _ANE
Color the picture.

Find and circle the letter 'm.' Can you find all 5?

Write the missing upper or lowercase letter.

M__ __m

__m M__

Circle the moons that have the letter 'm' inside.

Draw a line while connecting the 'm' letters to find your way across the maze!

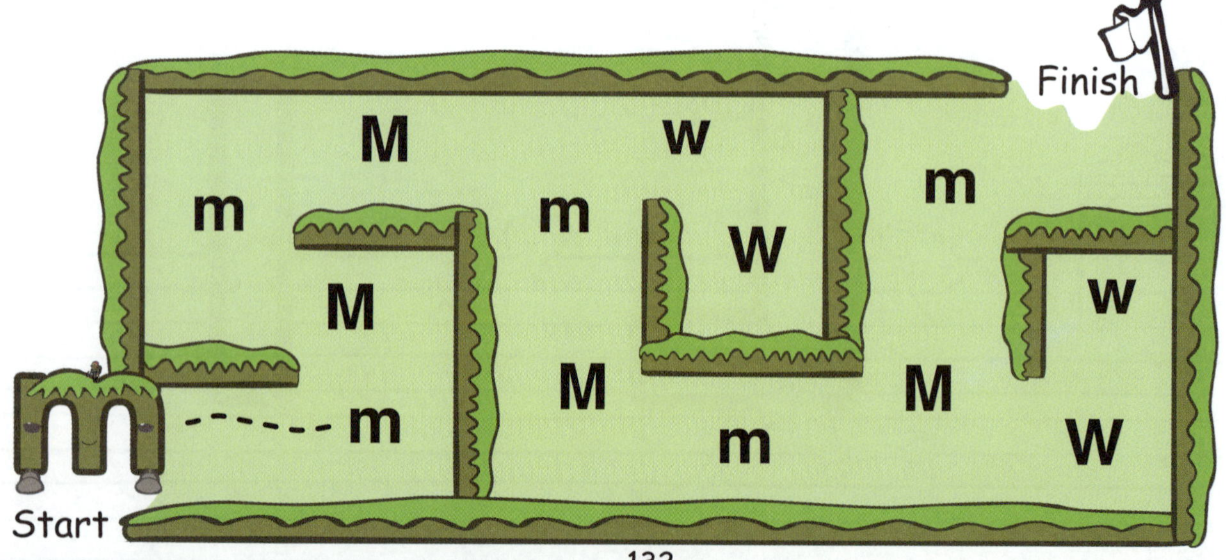

Find and circle the letter 'n.' Can you find all 5?

Circle the matching letters in each row.

M	m	n	m
N	n	n	u
L	l	i	l
N	m	n	n

Connect the lowercase 'n' letters to the uppercase 'N.'

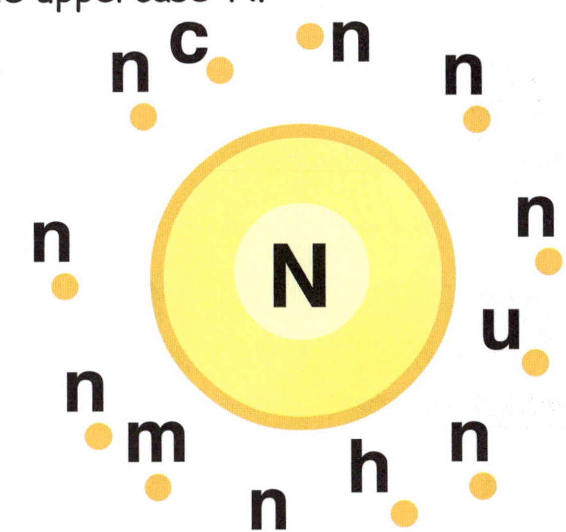

Complete the pattern below:

Find and circle the letter 'o.' Can you find all 5?

Draw a line to match the uppercase & lowercase letters.

M	**n**
N	**O**
o	**m**

Fill in the missing 'O' letters.

Color the picture.

Find and circle the letter 'p.' Can you find all 5?

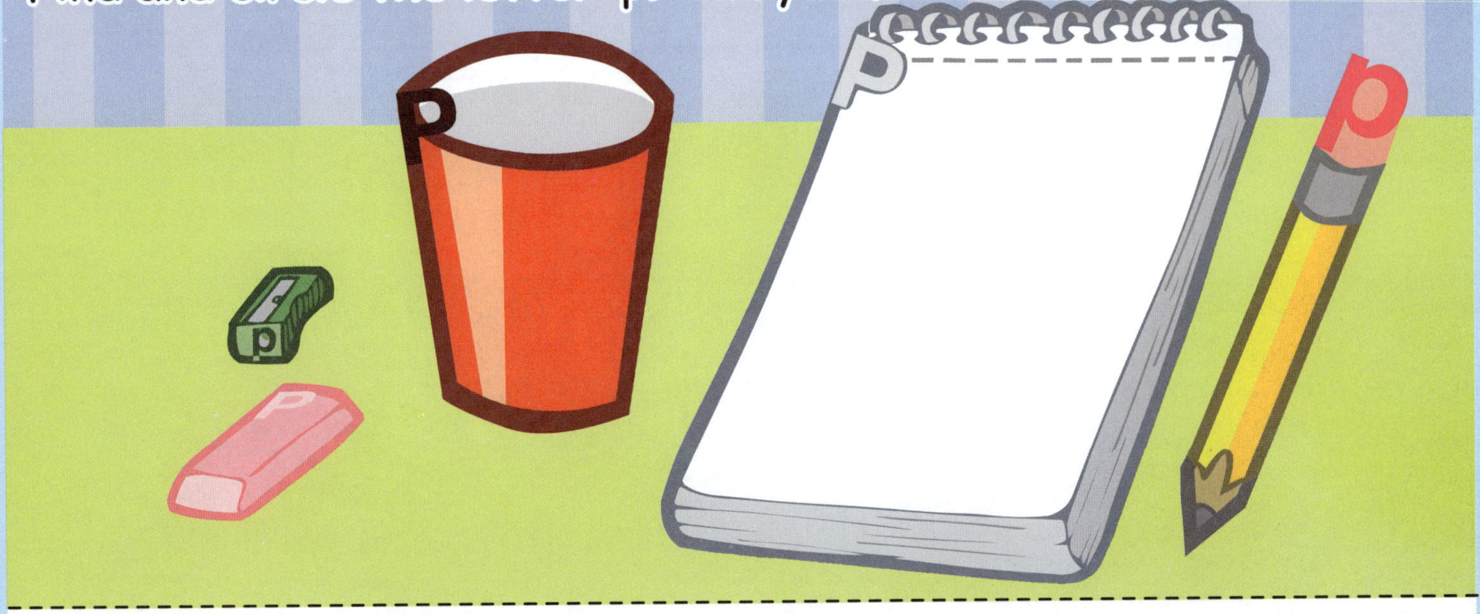

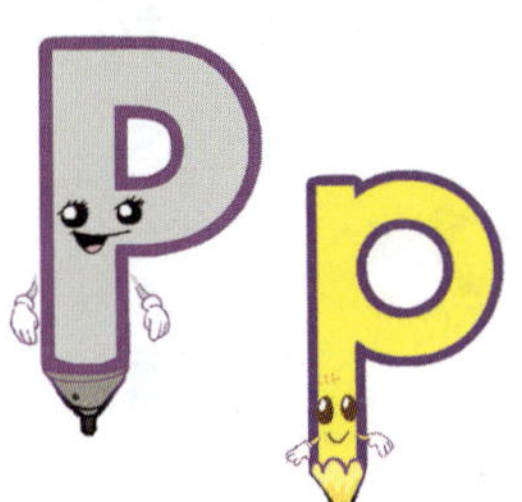

Write the missing upper or lowercase letter.

P___ ___p

___p P___

Circle the telephones that have the 'p' inside.

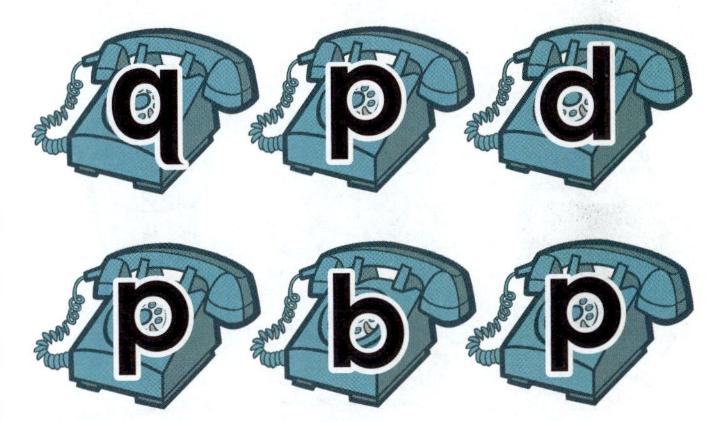

Draw a line while connecting the 'p' letters to find your way across the maze!

Start

Finish

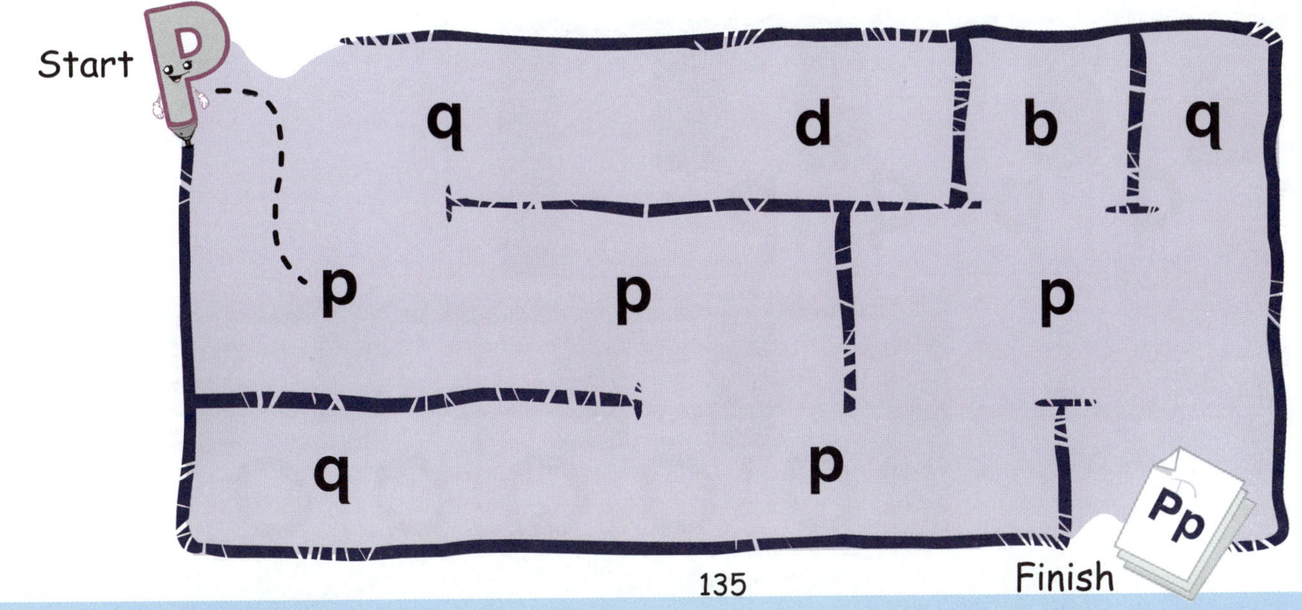

Find and circle the letter 'q.' Can you find all 5?

Circle the matching letters in each row.

Connect the lowercase 'q' letters to the uppercase 'Q.'

Complete the pattern below:

Find and circle the letter 'r.' Can you find all 5?

Draw a line to match the uppercase & lowercase letters.

p	Q
q	P
R	r

Fill in the missing 'R' letters.

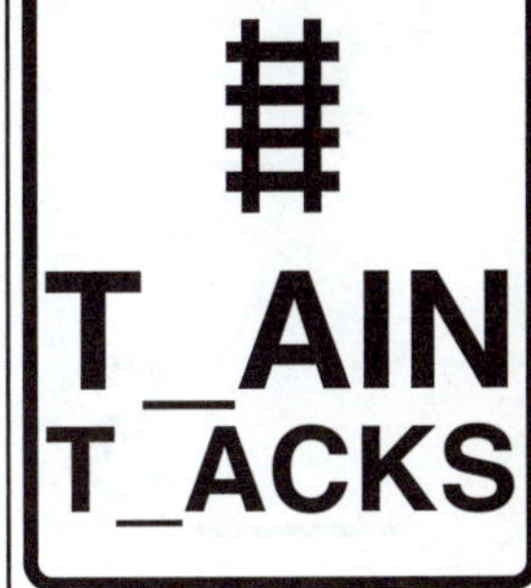

Color the picture.

Find and circle the letter 's.' Can you find all 5?

Write the missing upper or lowercase letter.

__s S__

Circle the sandwiches that have the 's' inside.

s c s

Draw a line while connecting the 's' letters to find your way across the maze!

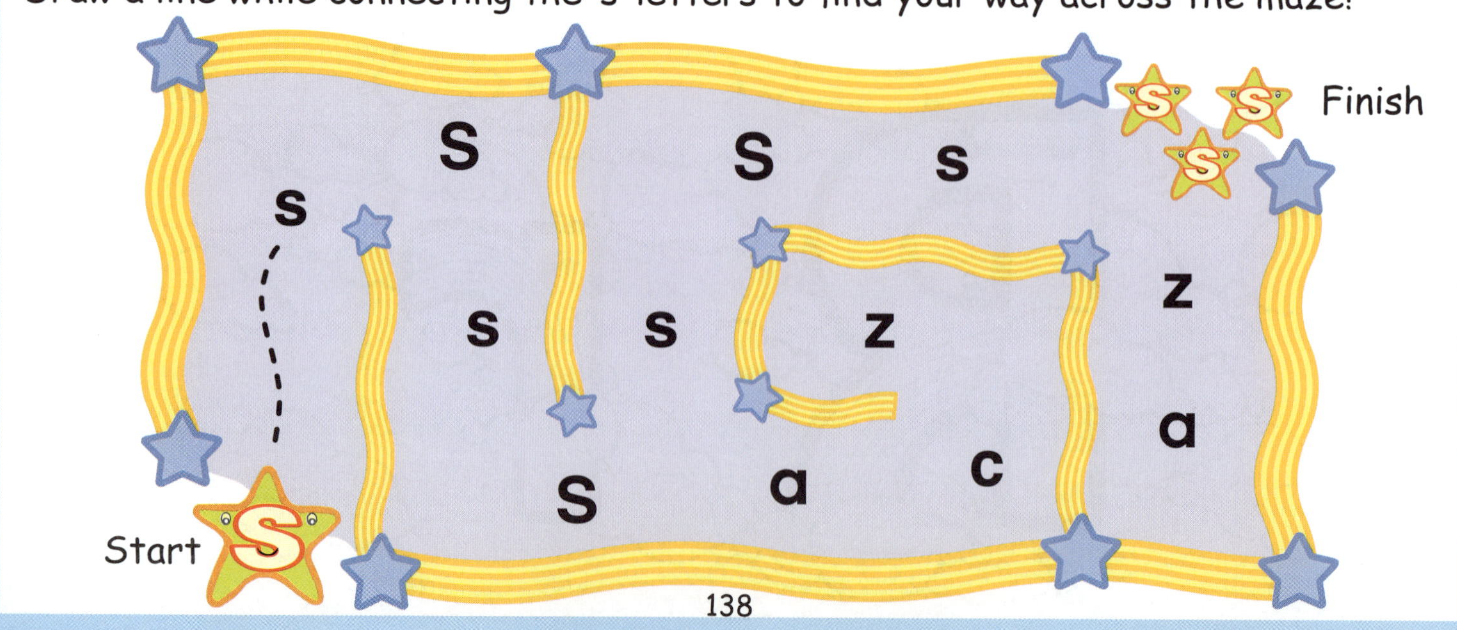

Find and circle the letter 't.' Can you find all 5?

Circle the matching letters in each row.

Connect the lowercase 't' letters to the uppercase 'T.'

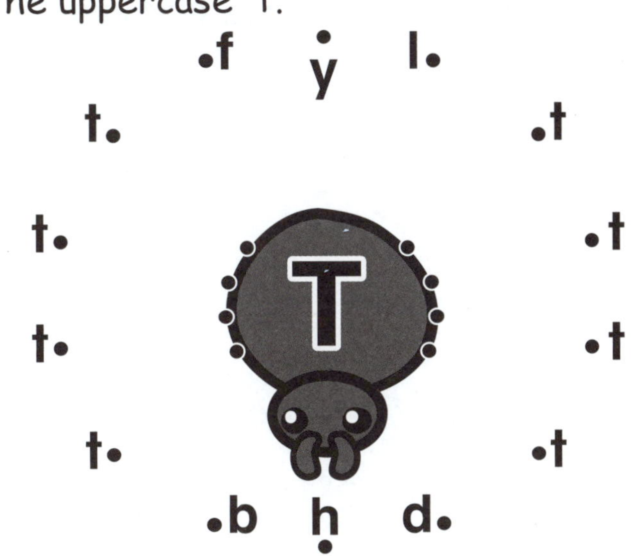

Complete the patterns below:

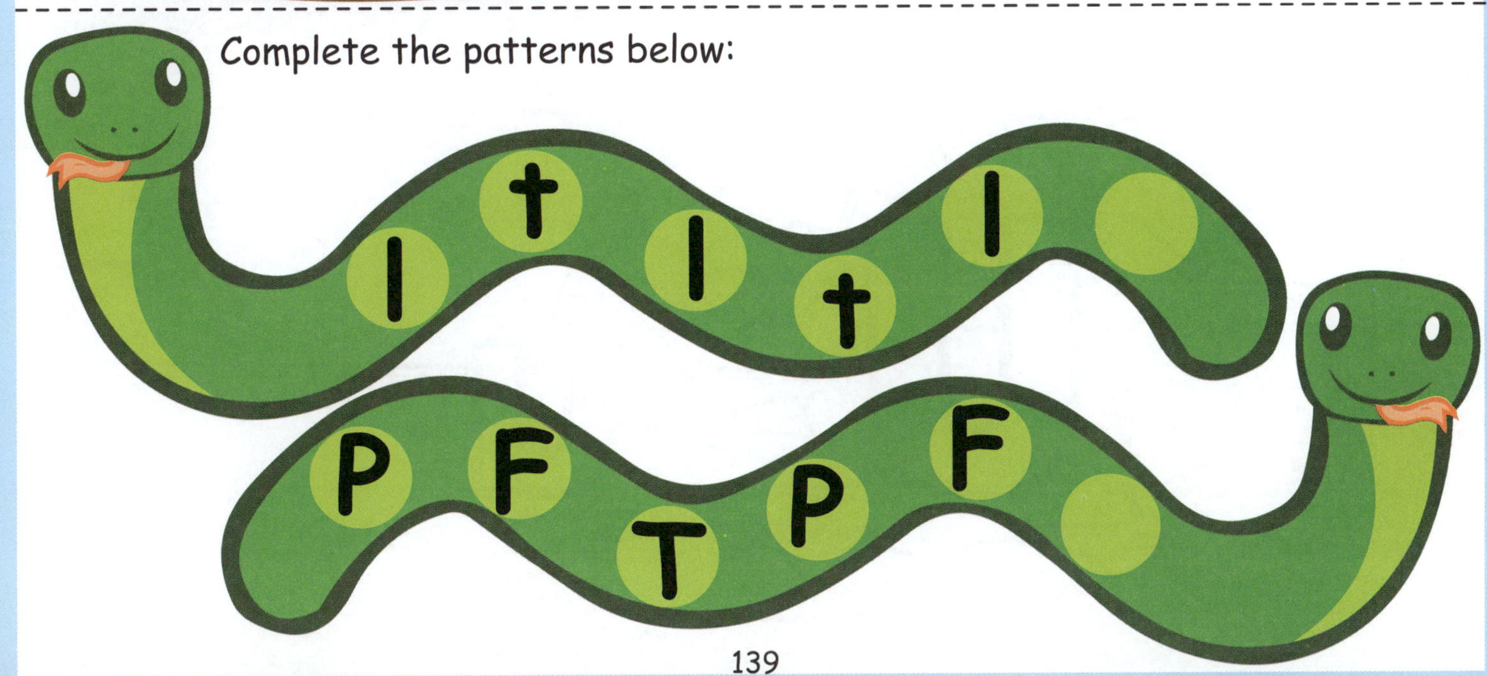

Find and circle the letter 'u.' Can you find all 5?

Draw a line to match the uppercase & lowercase letters.

S	s
t	u
U	T

Fill in the missing 'U' letters.

Color the picture.

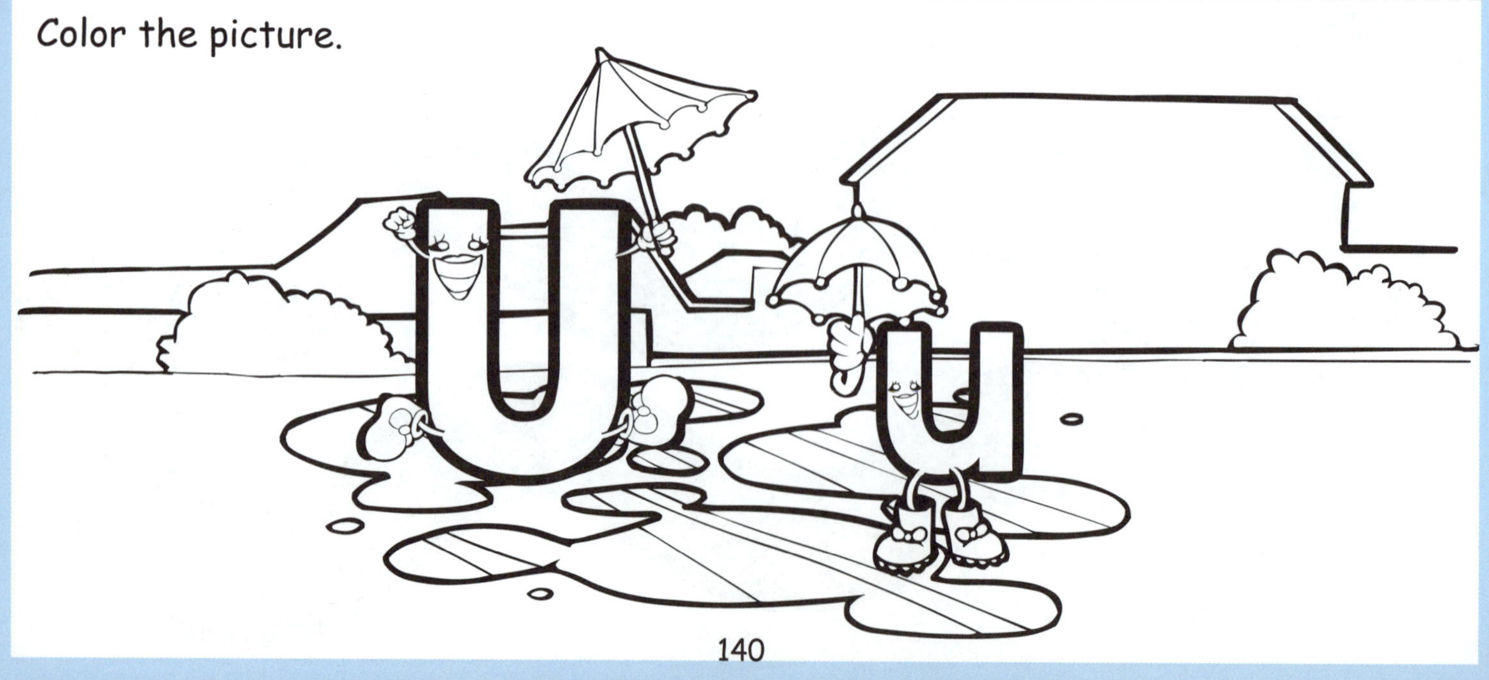

Find and circle the letter 'v.' Can you find all 5?

Write the missing upper or lowercase letter.

V___ ___v

___v V___

Circle the vases that have the 'v' inside.

Draw a line while connecting the 'v' letters to find your way across the maze!

Find and circle the letter 'w.' Can you find all 5?

Circle the matching letters in each row.

Connect the lowercase 'w' letters to the uppercase 'W.'

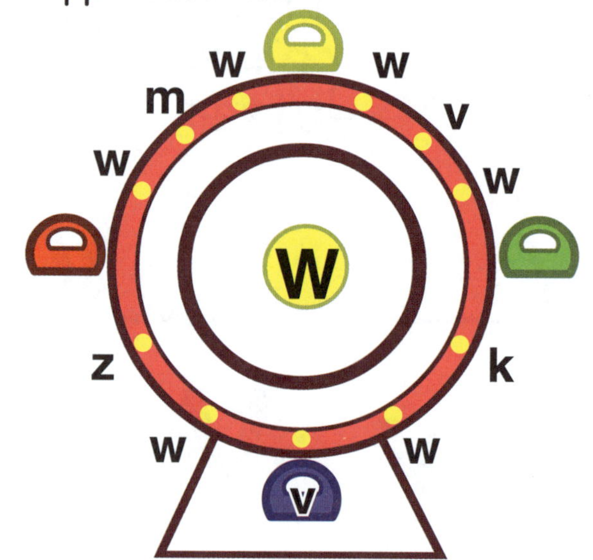

Complete the pattern below:

Find and circle the letter 'x.' Can you find all 5?
Draw a line to match the uppercase & lowercase letters.
V
W
X
w
x
v
Fill in the missing 'X' letters.
TE_AS
NO
_ING
_ING
Color the picture.

Find and circle the letter 'y.' Can you find all 5?

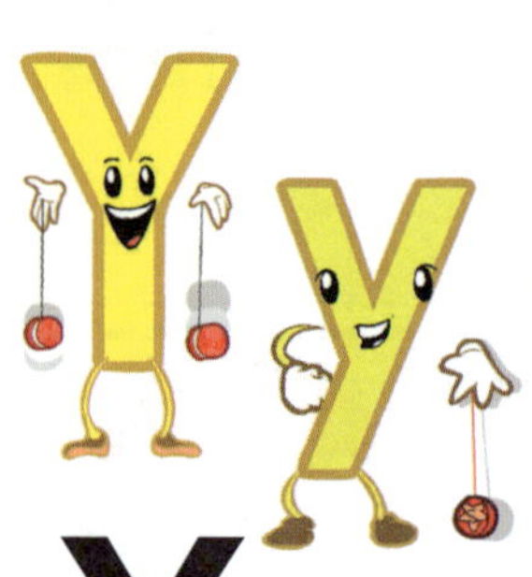

Write the missing upper or lowercase letter.

Y__ __y

__y Y__

Circle the yarn balls that have the 'y' inside.

Draw a line while connecting the 'y' letters to find your way across the maze!

Start

L y Y y Finish

h Y u Y y

y V T

Find and circle the letter 'z.' Can you find all 5?

Circle the matching Letters in each row.

Connect the lowercase 'z' letters to the uppercase 'Z.'

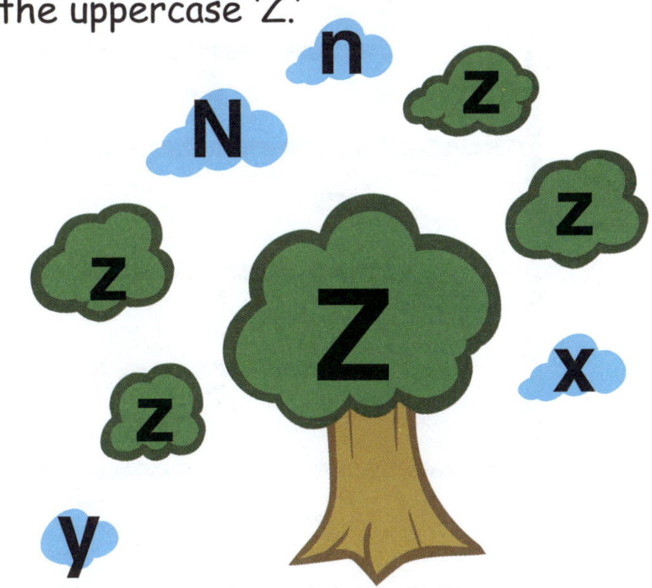

Complete the patterns below:

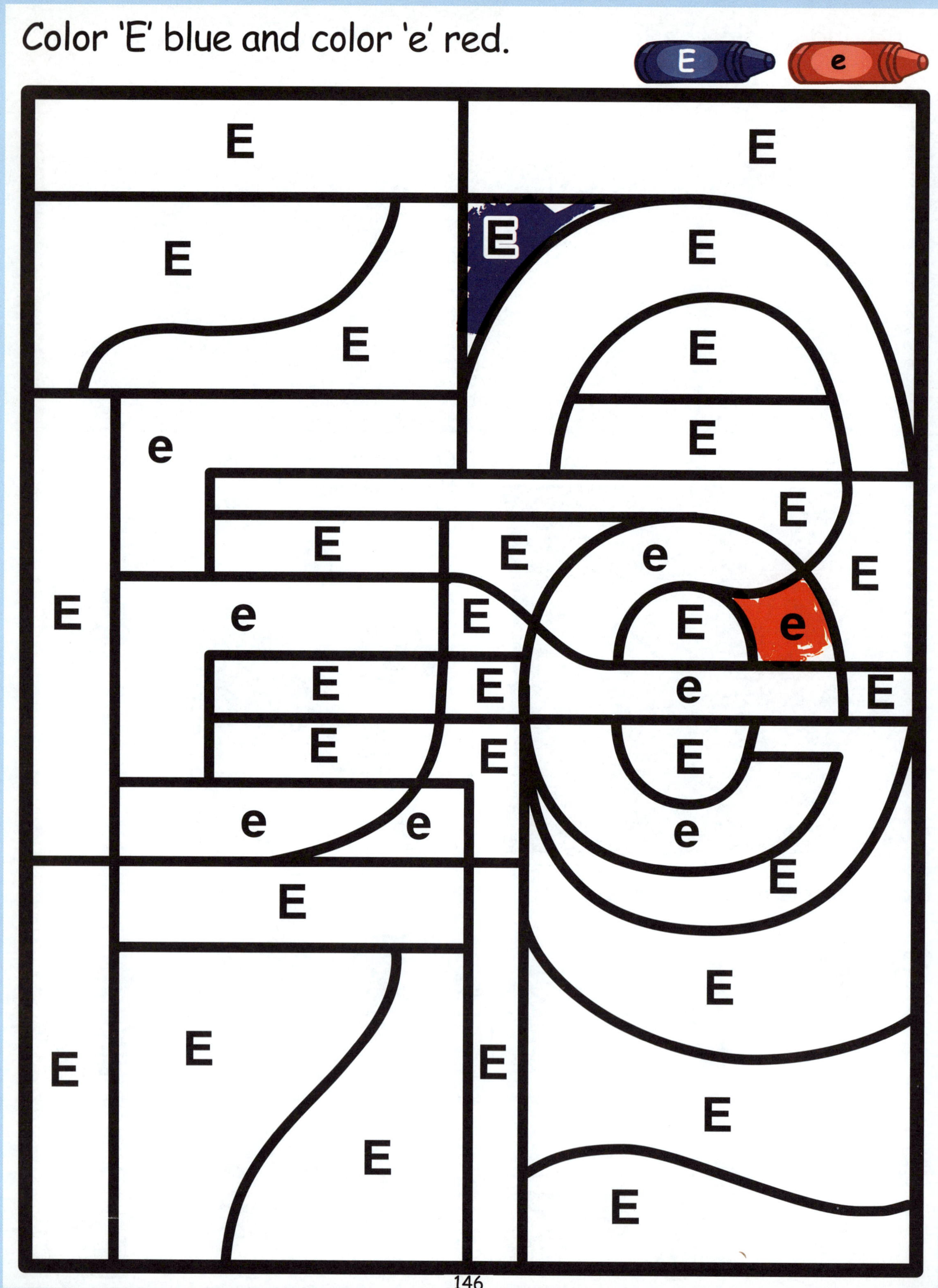
Color 'E' blue and color 'e' red.
E
e
©2019 Kathy Oxley. Meet the Letters and all related titles, logos and characters are trademarks of Preschool Prep Company®

Color 'B' green and color 'b' yellow.

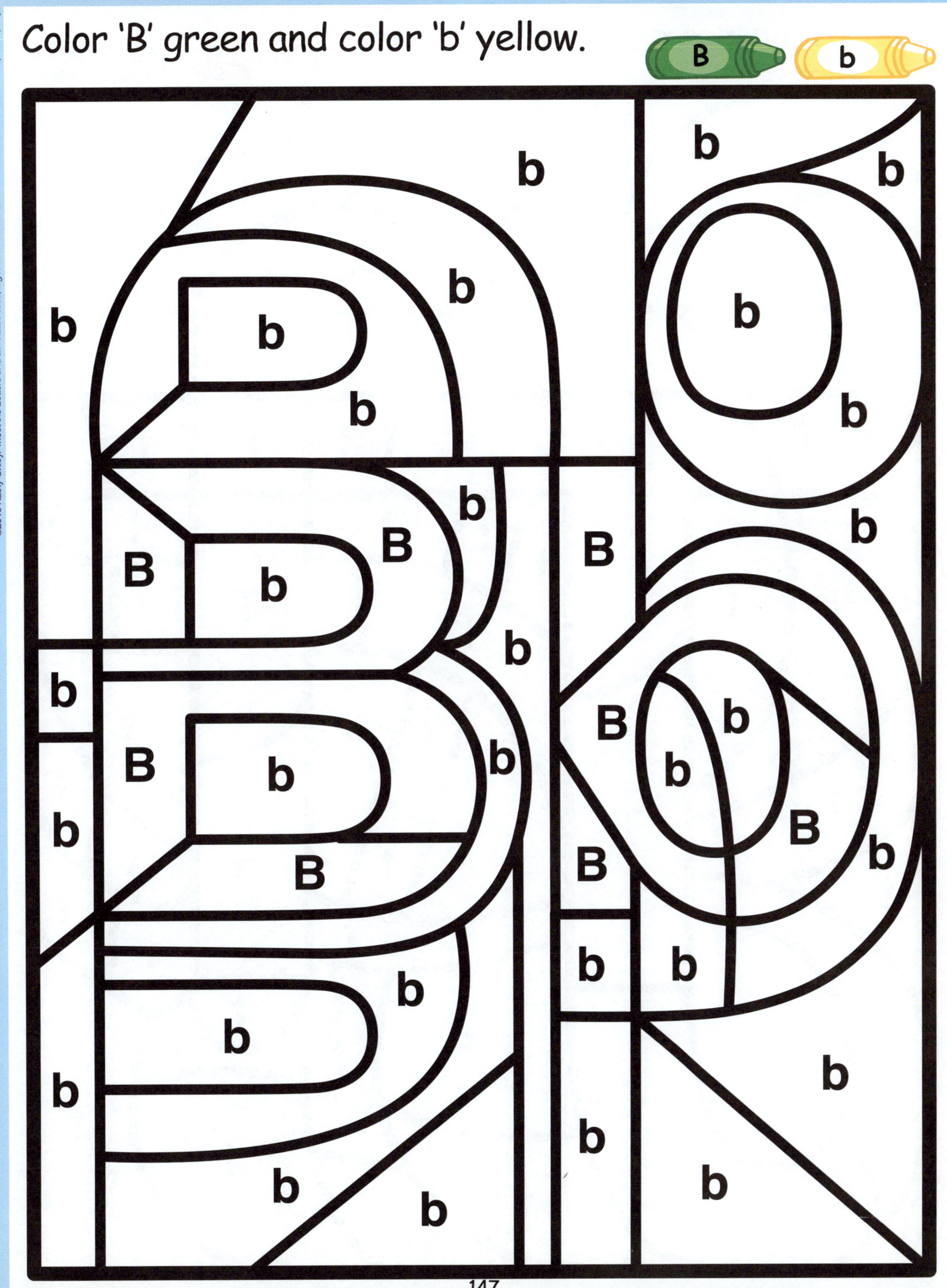

Color 'T' orange and color 't' purple.

Color 'G' yellow and color 'g' blue.

G g

G G G G G G G G G g G G G g G G g G g g G g G G G g G G G g G G G G g G g G G G G G G G G G G G G G G G G G G G G G G G G G G

Color 'R' green and color 'r' yellow.

R r

r r r r r r r r R R r r r R r r R R r r r R r r R r r r r r r r r r r r r r r r r r r r r r r r

Color 'N' red and color 'n' purple.
N
n

Color 'A' red and color 'a' purple.

A a

Color ‘U’ orange and color ‘u’ yellow.

U u

u u u

u

u u

u

u u

u u

U

U

u

u

u

u U

u

u U

U

u

u u

u

u

u

u

u

Color 'D' orange and color 'd' purple.

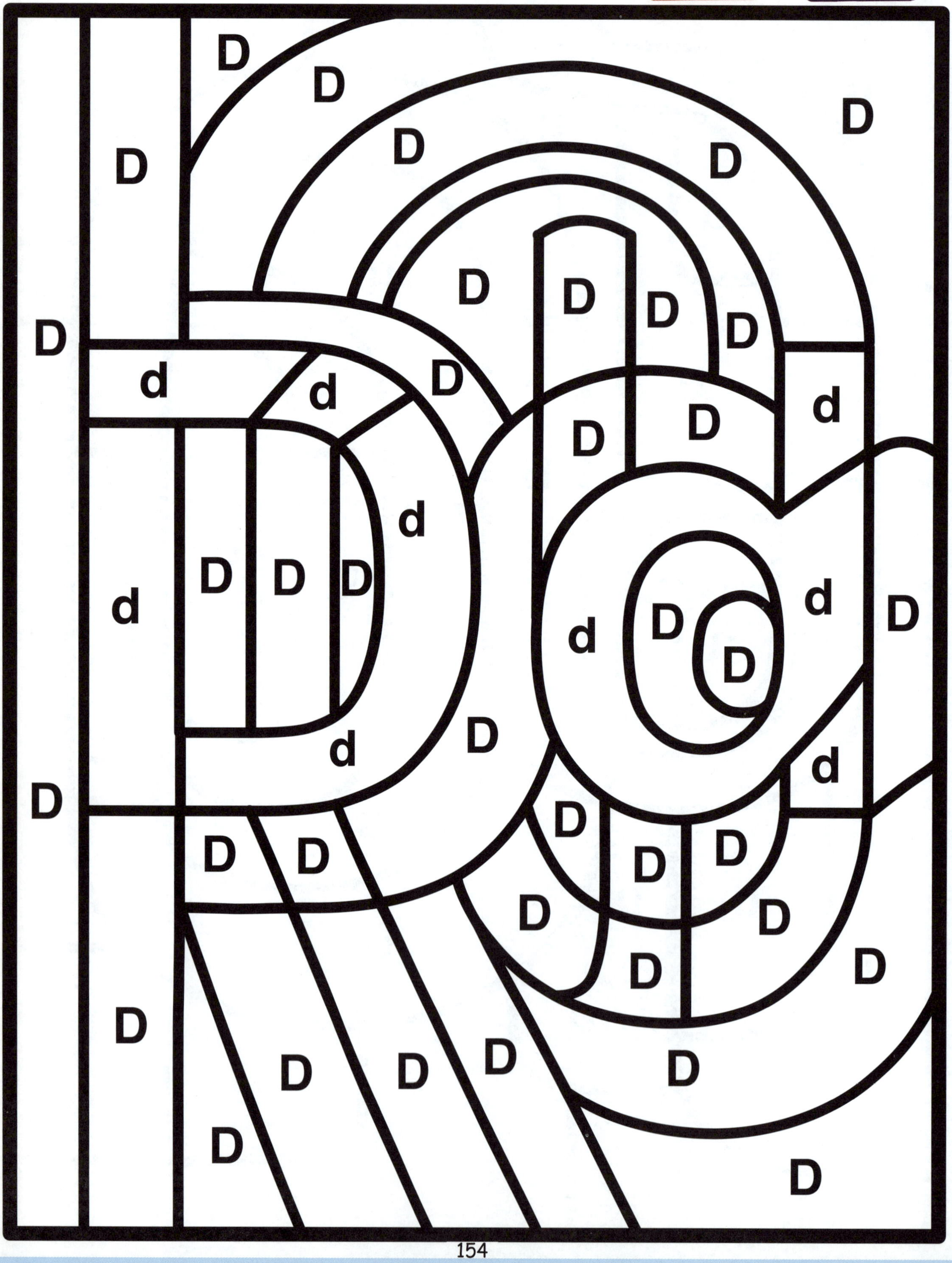

D d

Color 'J' orange and color 'j' blue.

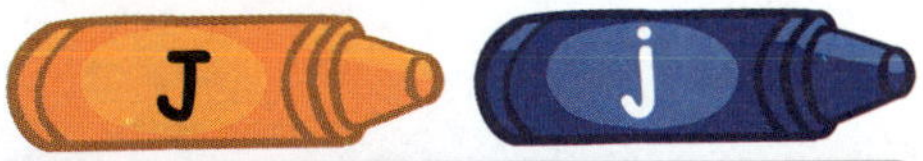

J
j

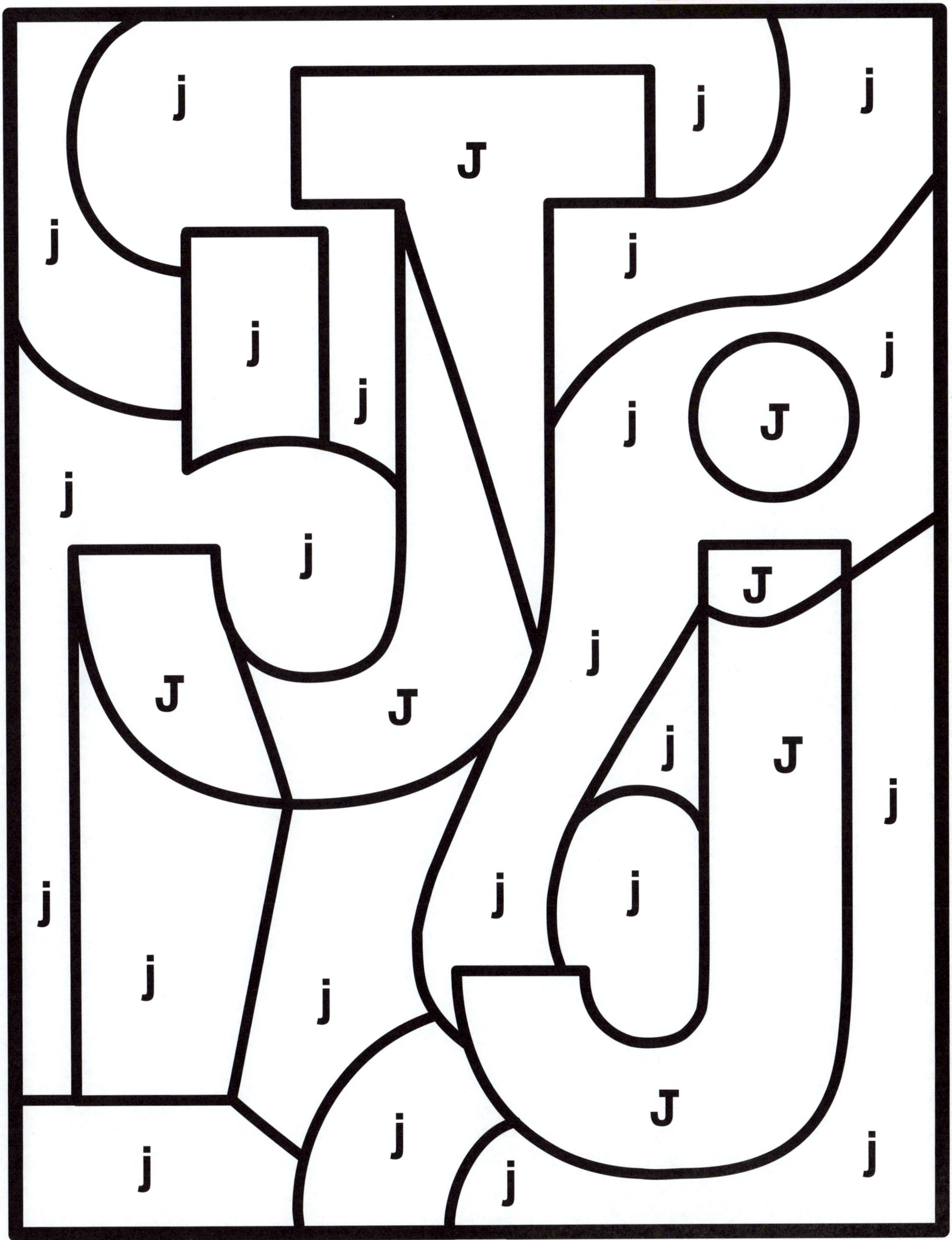

j
j
j
J
j
j
j
j
j
j
J
j
j
J
j
J
J
j
J
j
j
j
j
j
j
J
j
j
j
j

Meet the Numbers™

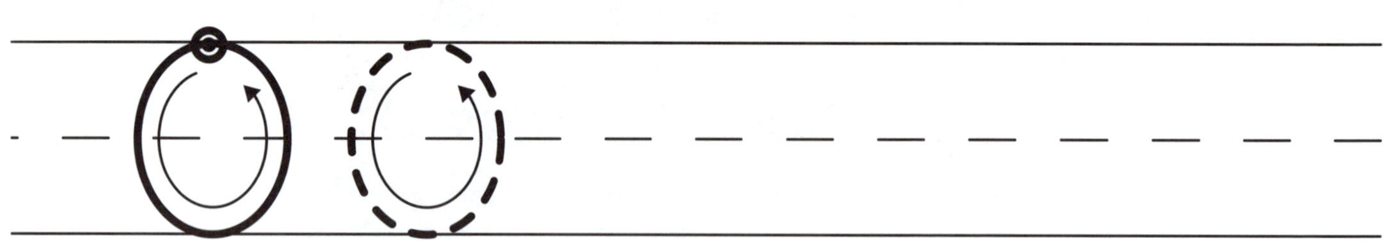

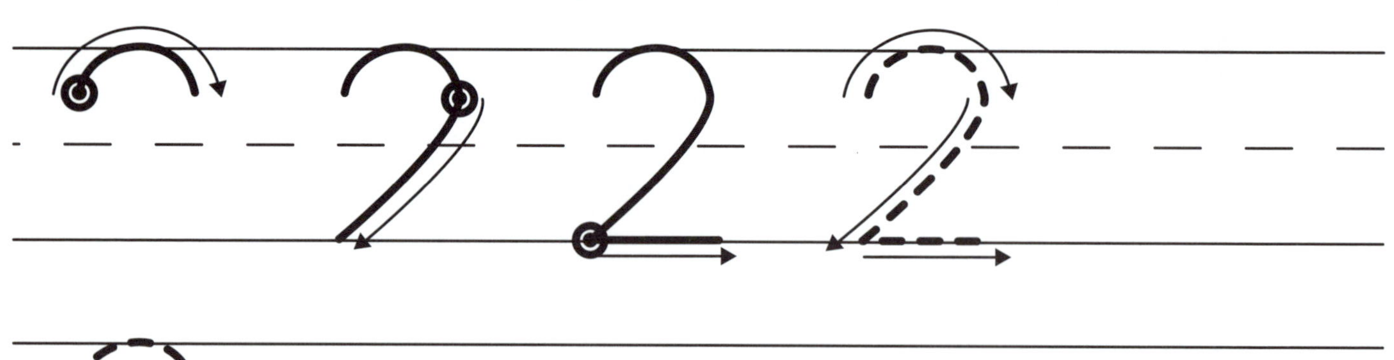

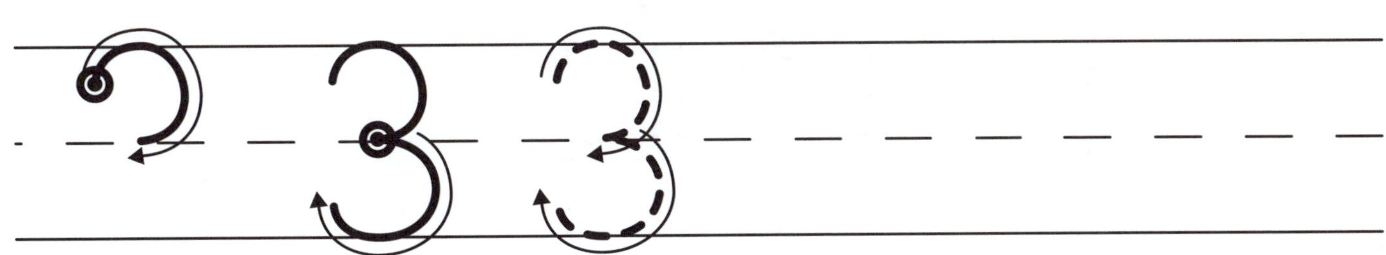

STOP
4

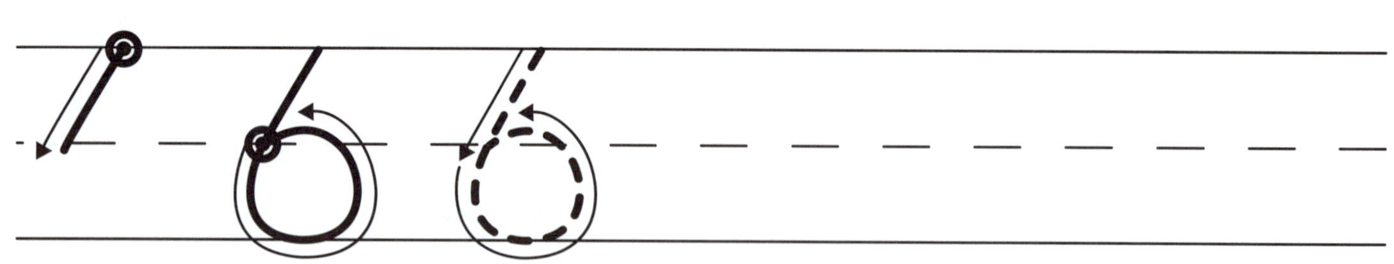

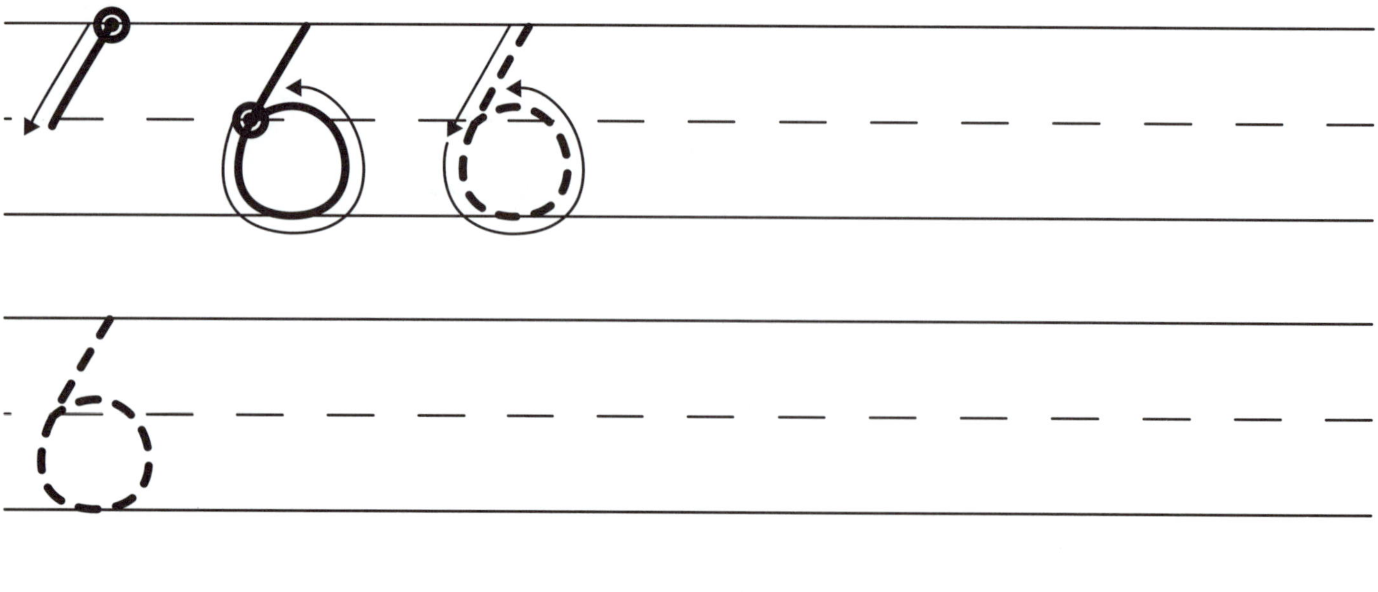

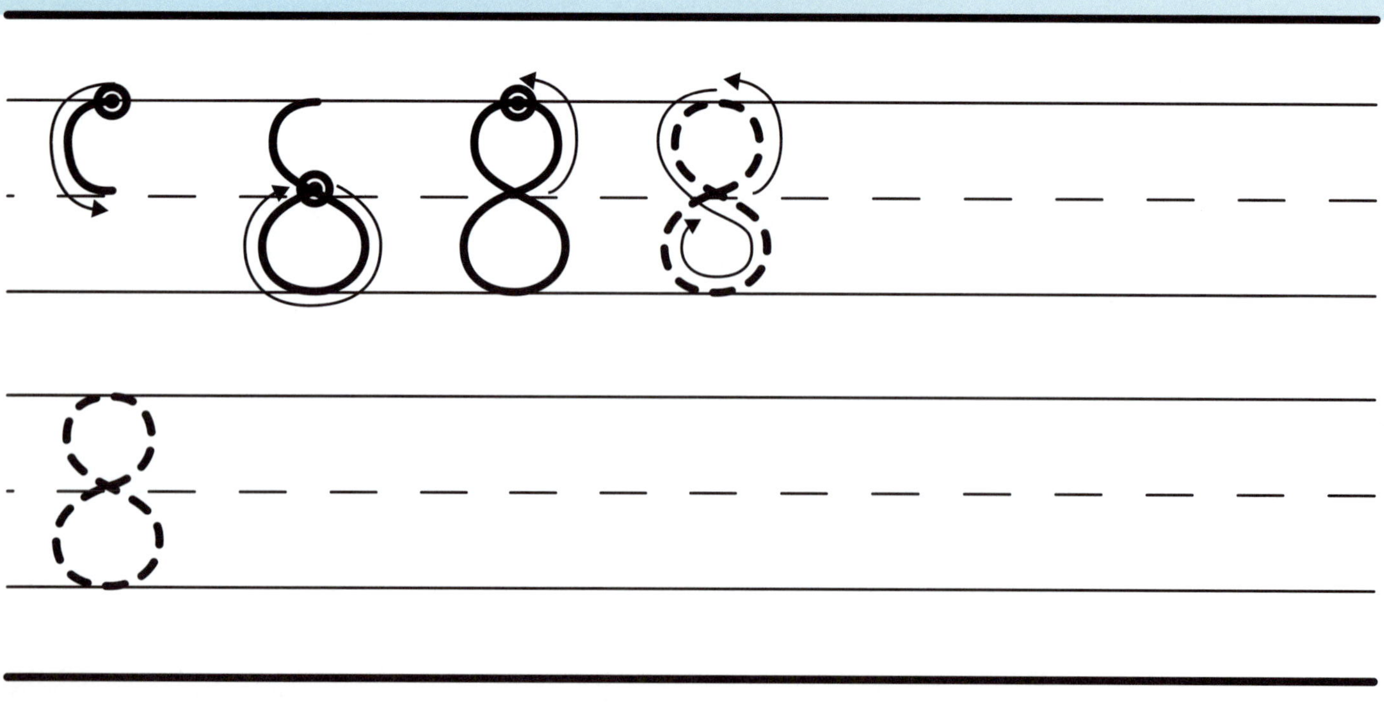

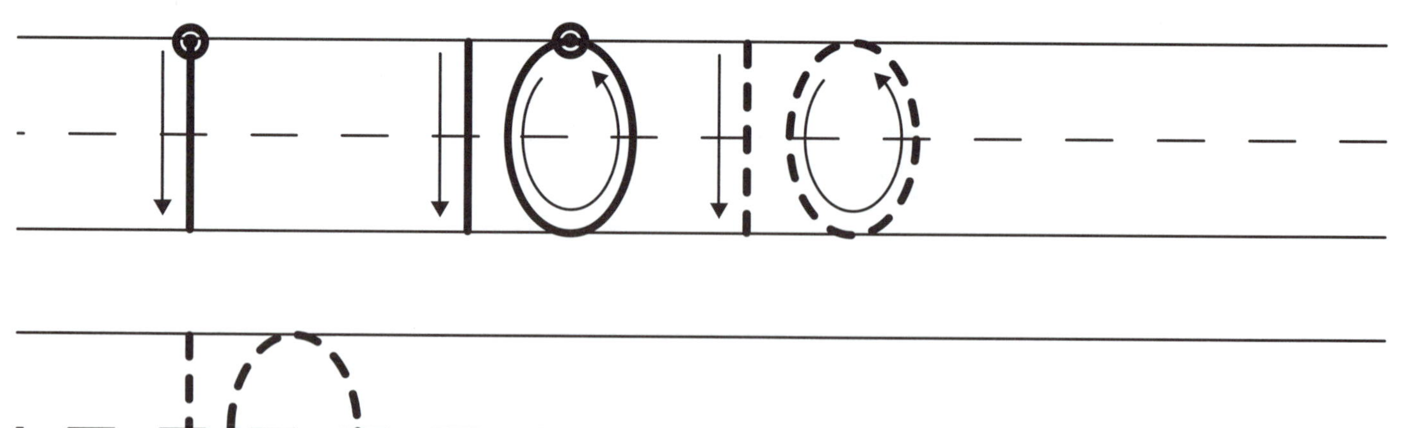

Connect the dots starting with 'A,' connect the dots starting with '1' and then color the picture.

Connect the dots starting with 'A,' connect the dots starting with '1' and then color the picture.

Connect the dots starting with 'A,' connect the dots starting with '1' and then color the picture.

Connect the dots starting with 'A,' connect the dots starting with '1' and then color the picture.

Connect the dots starting with 'A,' connect the dots starting with '1' and then color the picture.

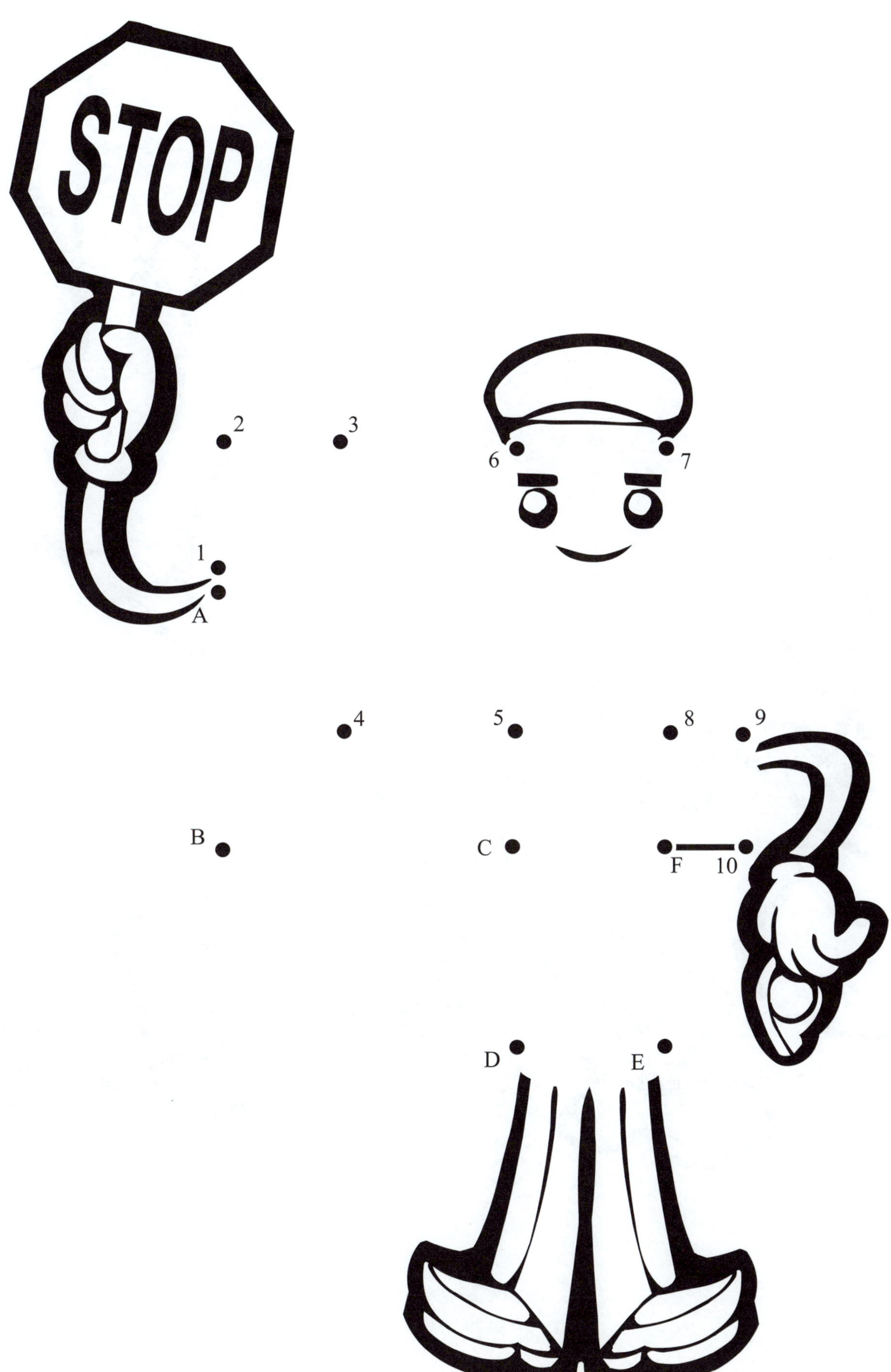

Connect the dots starting with 'A,' connect the dots starting with '1' and then color the picture.

Connect the dots starting with 'A,' connect the dots starting with '1' and then color the picture.

Connect the dots starting with 'A,' connect the dots starting with '1' and then color the picture.

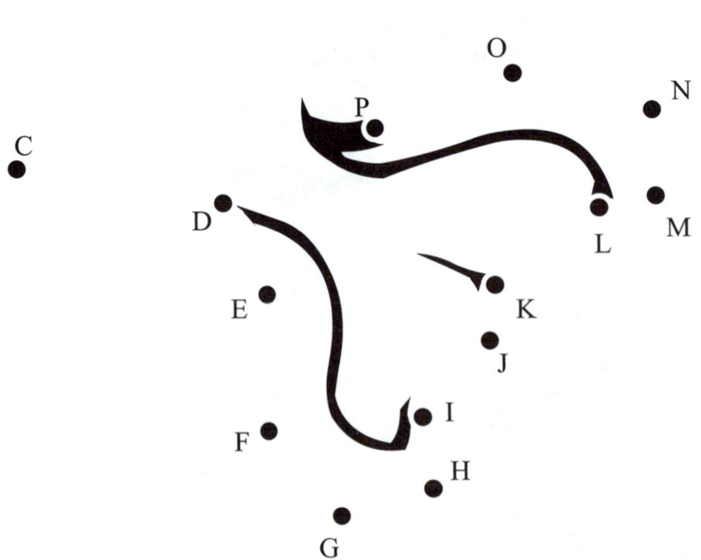

Connect the dots starting with 'A,' connect the dots starting with '1' and then color the picture.

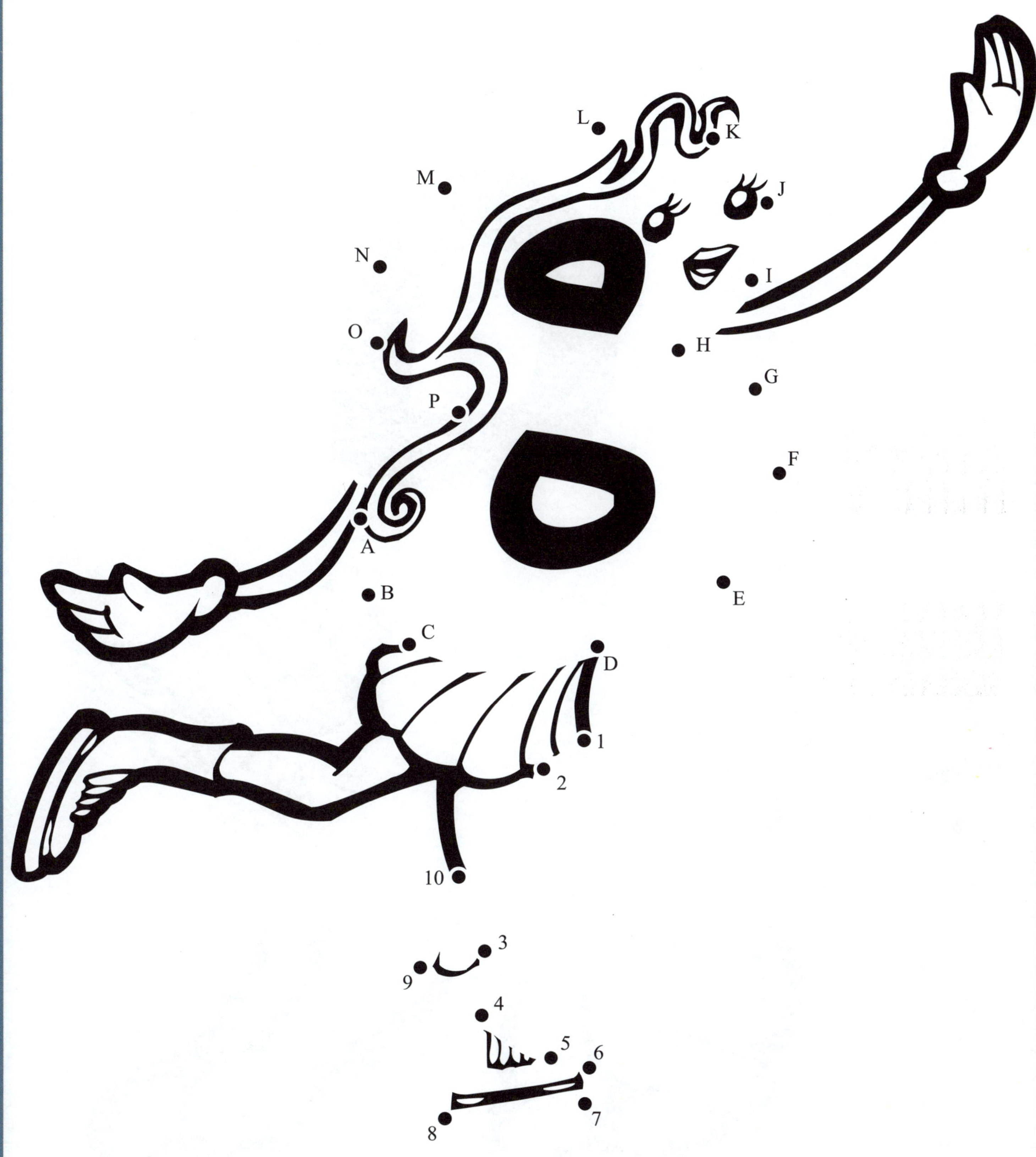

Connect the dots starting with 'A,' connect the dots starting with '1' and then color the picture.

Connect the dots starting with 'A,' connect the dots starting with '1' and then color the picture.

Circle the correct number of objects in each row.

1

2

3

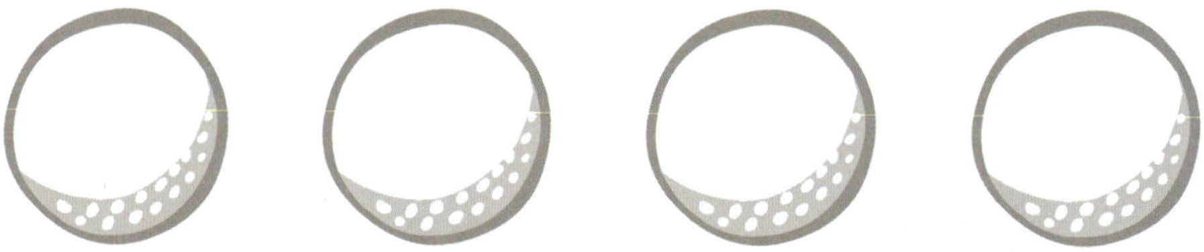

4

5

Circle the correct number of objects in each row.

6

7

8

9

10

Draw a line to match the number with the number of objects in each set.

8

4

2

Draw a line to match the number with the number of objects in each set.

3

10

5

Draw a line to match the number with the number of objects in each set.

1

7

9

Draw a line to match the number with the number of objects in each set.

6

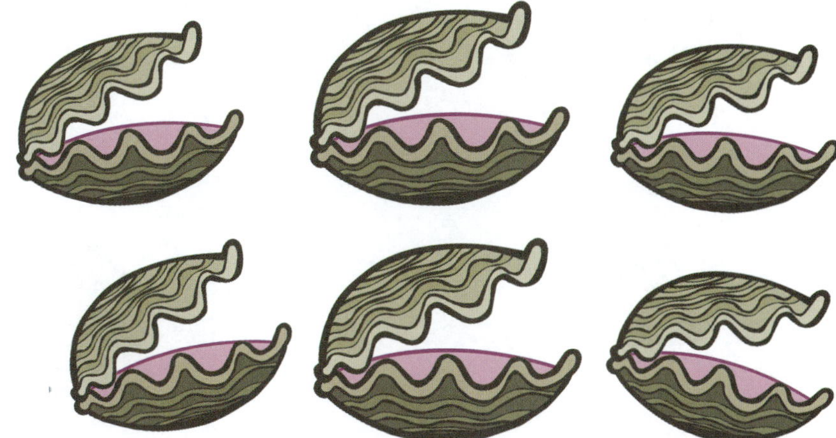

2

0

Draw a line to match the number with the number of objects in each set.

7

10

4

Draw a line to match the number with the number of objects in each set.

3

0

8

Draw a line to match the number with the number of objects in each set.

6

1

9

Draw a line to match the number with the number of objects in each set.

4

9

3

Draw a line to match the number with the number of objects in each set.

1

3

5

Draw a line to match the number with the number of objects in each set.

10

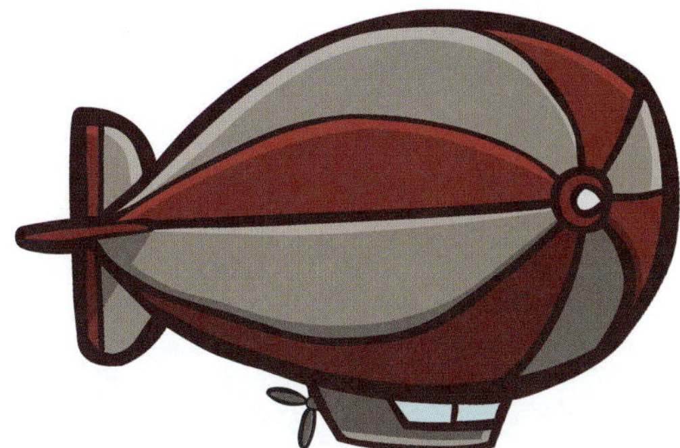

1

8

Circle the numbers.

b

8

4

q

a

6

j

3

7

Circle the numbers.

q

5

c

9

7

x

k

8

2

Circle the 5 things that are different in the 2 pictures.

Circle the 5 things that are different in the 2 pictures.

Circle the fruit with the <u>larger</u> number in each pair.

Circle the fruit with the larger number in each pair.

Circle the flower with the larger number in each pair.

Circle the candy with the smaller number in each pair.

Circle the animal with the smaller number in each pair.

Circle the animal with the smaller number in each pair.

Meet the
Shapes™

Trace & color the shape.

Draw a line while connecting the '**circle**' shapes to find your way across the maze.

Complete the character.

Trace & color the shape.

Color the '**diamond**' shapes to create a path across the page.

Complete the character.

Trace & color the shape.

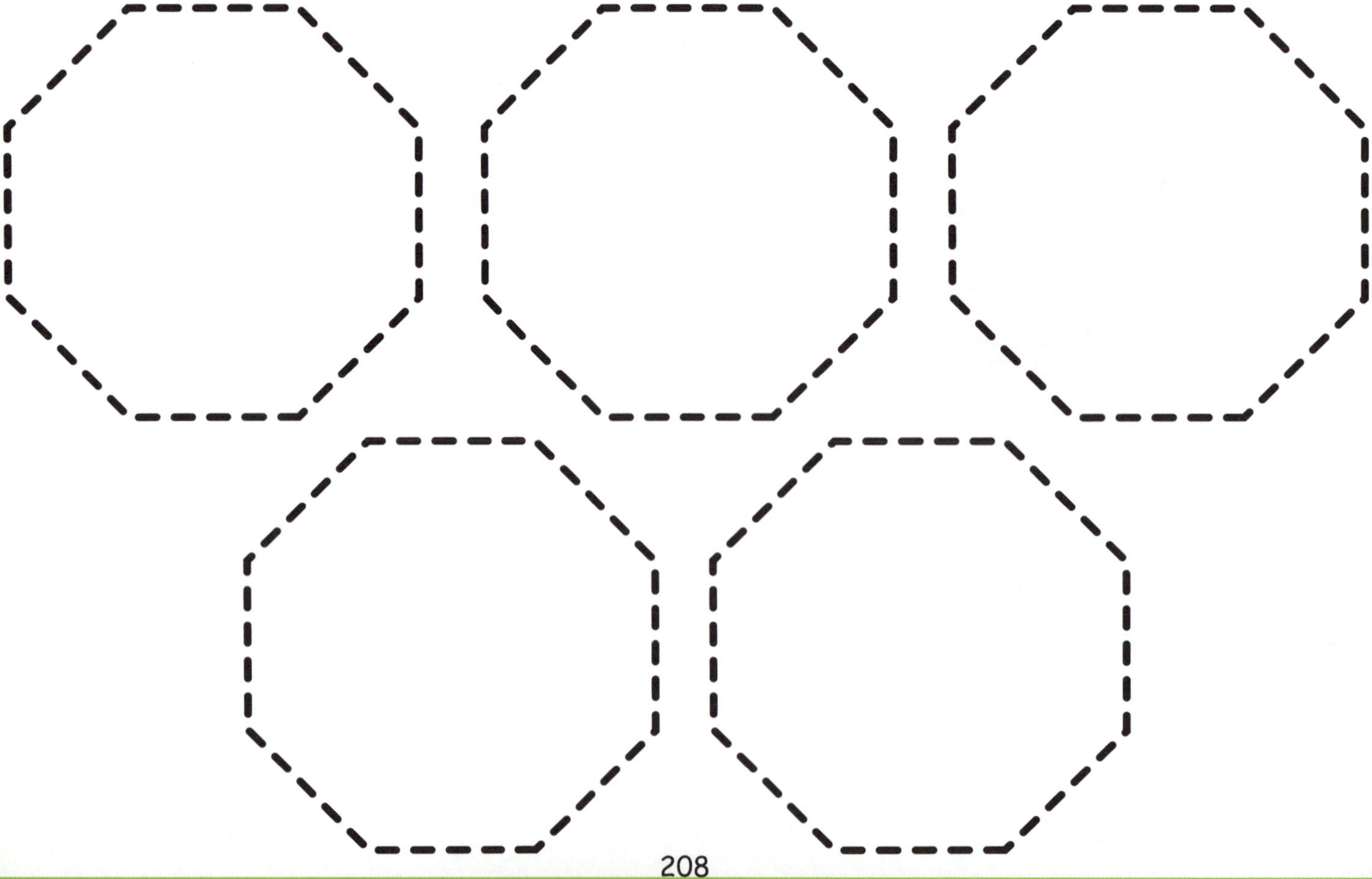

Draw a line while connecting the '**octagon**' shapes to find your way across the maze.

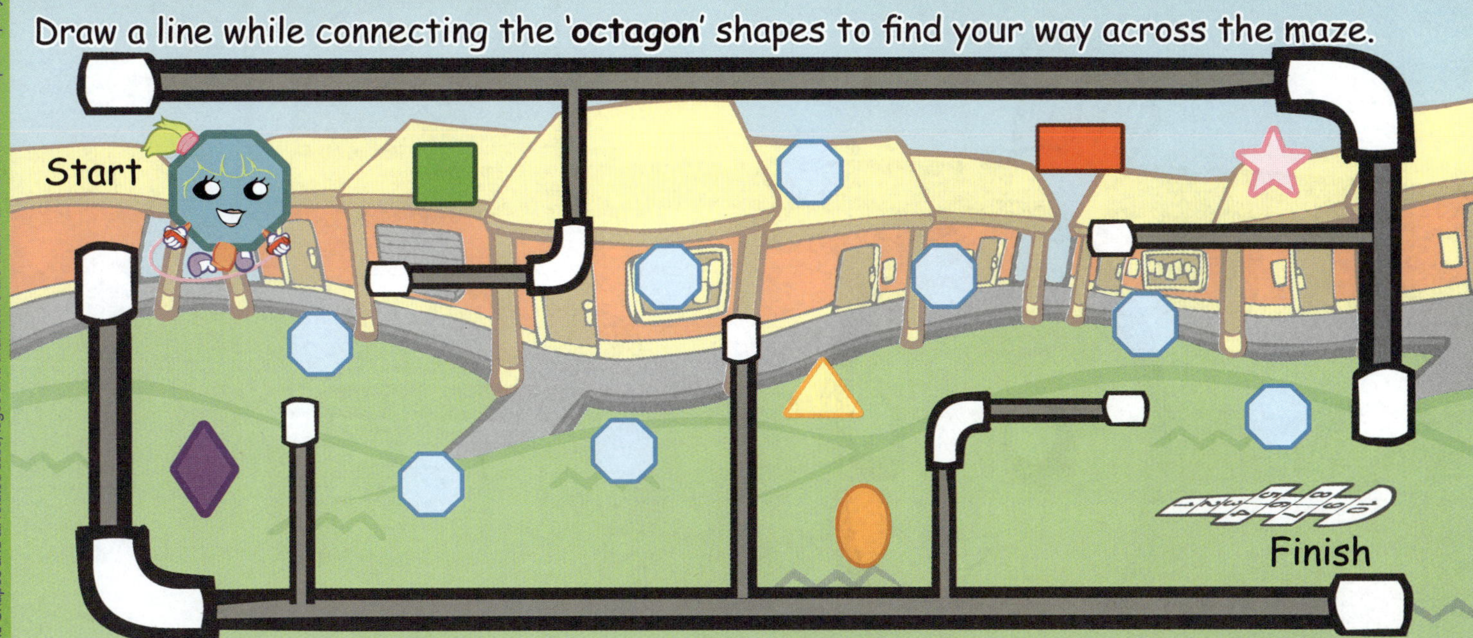

Complete the character.

Trace & color the shape.

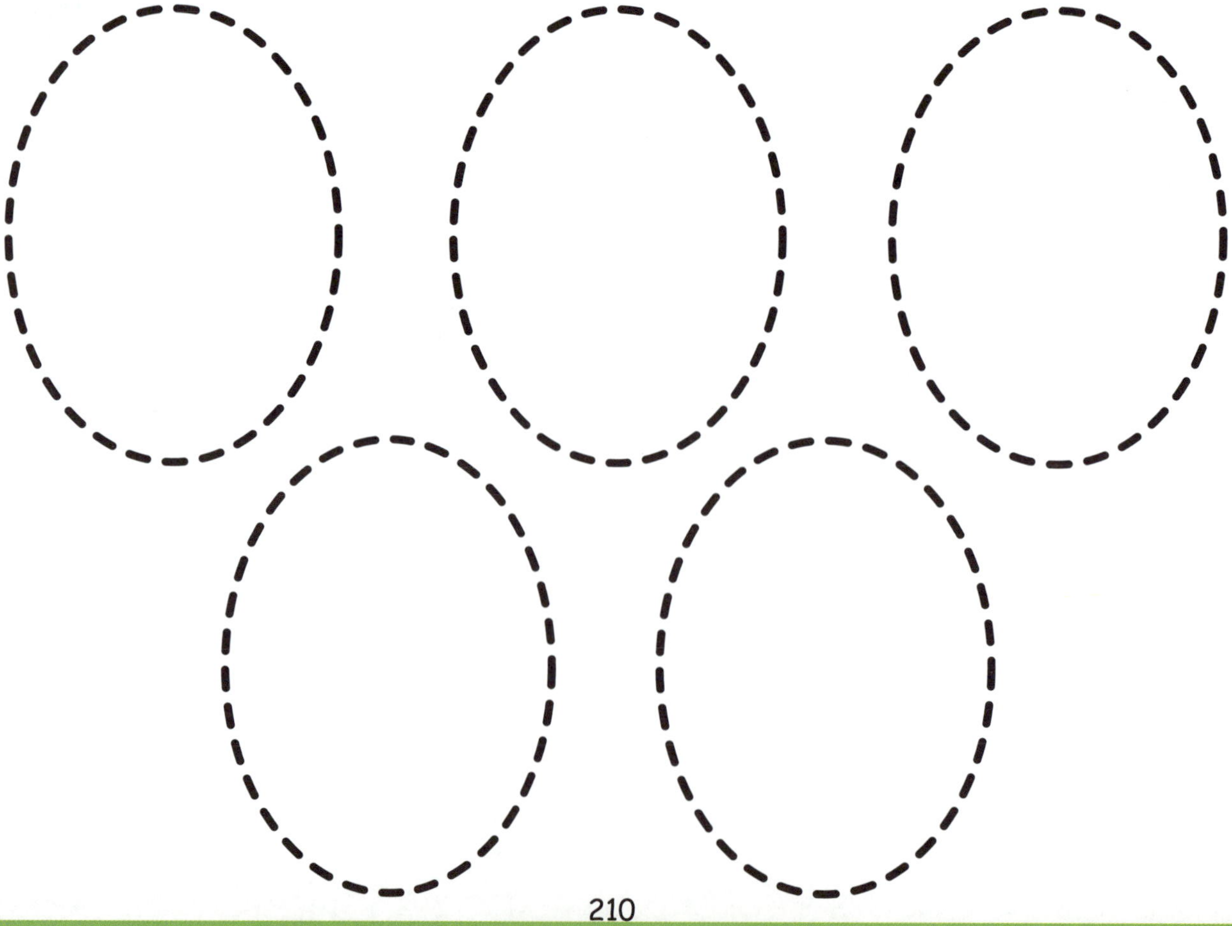

Color the '**oval**' shapes to create a path across the page.

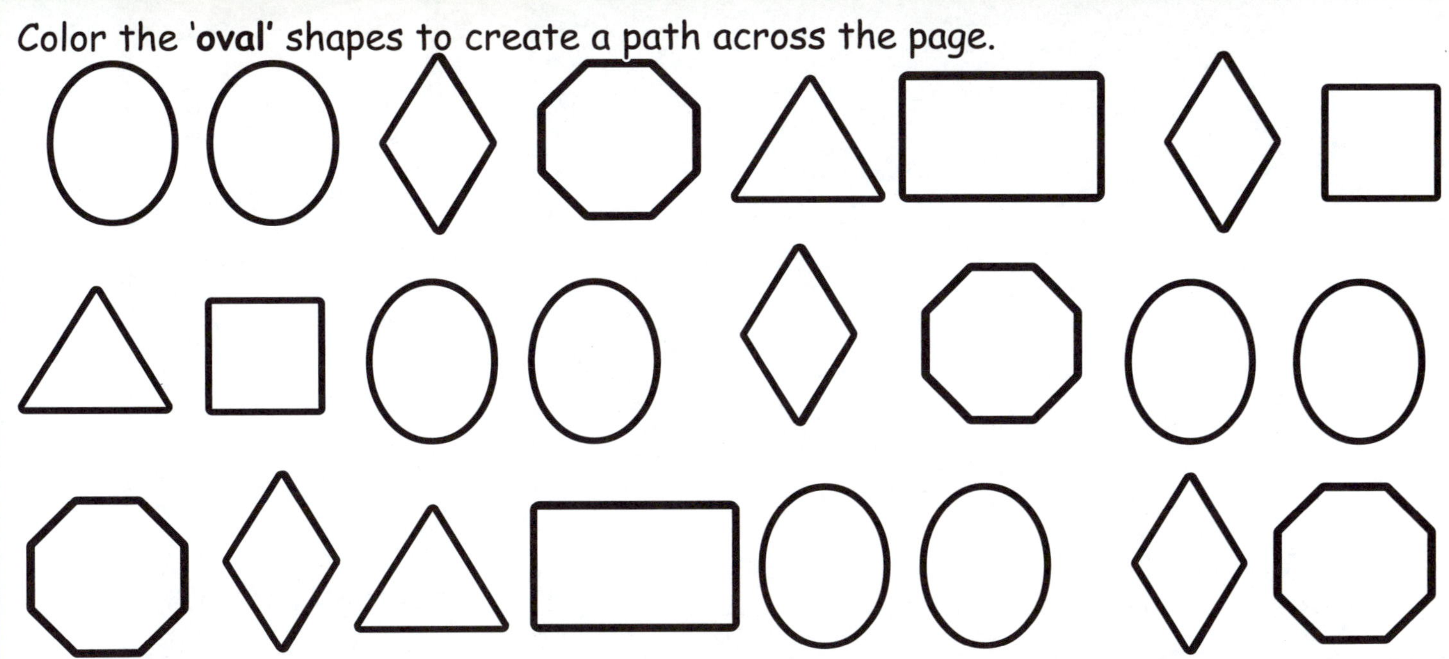

Complete the character.

Trace & color the shape.

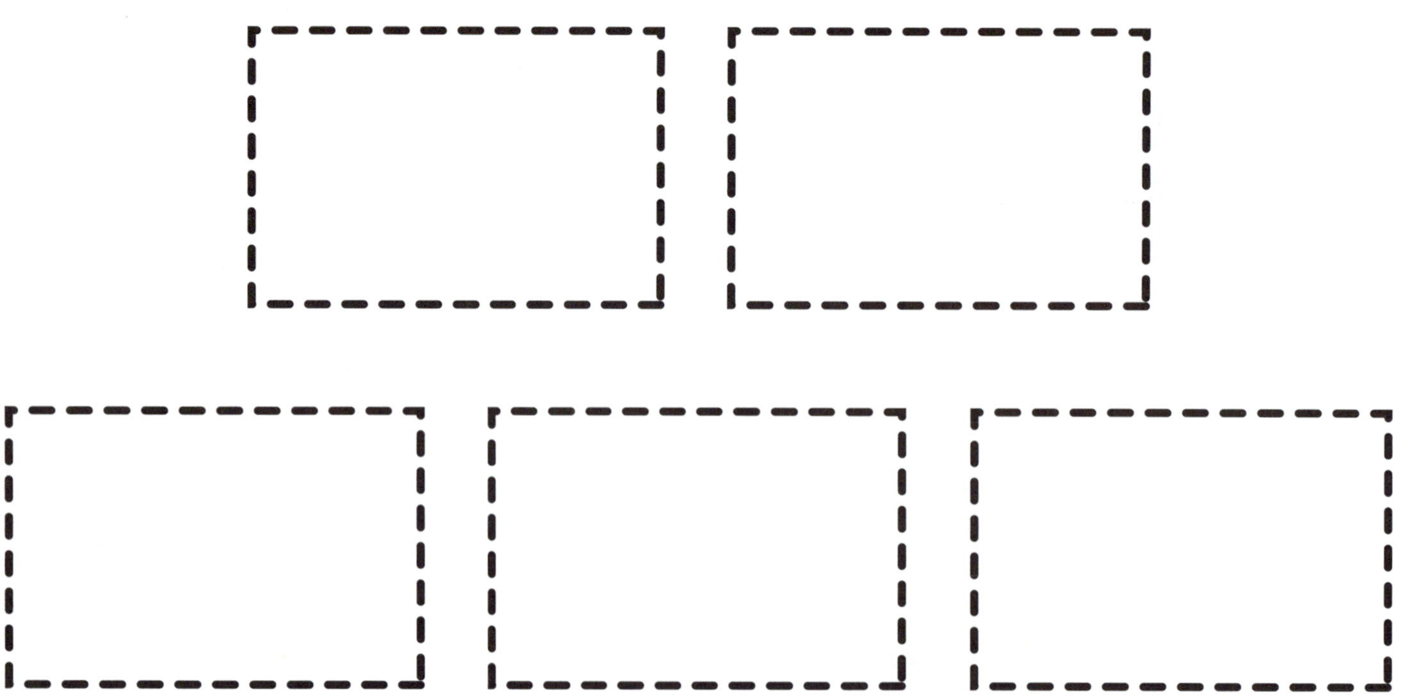

Draw a line while connecting the '**rectangle**' shapes to find your way across the maze.

Complete the character.

Trace & color the shape.

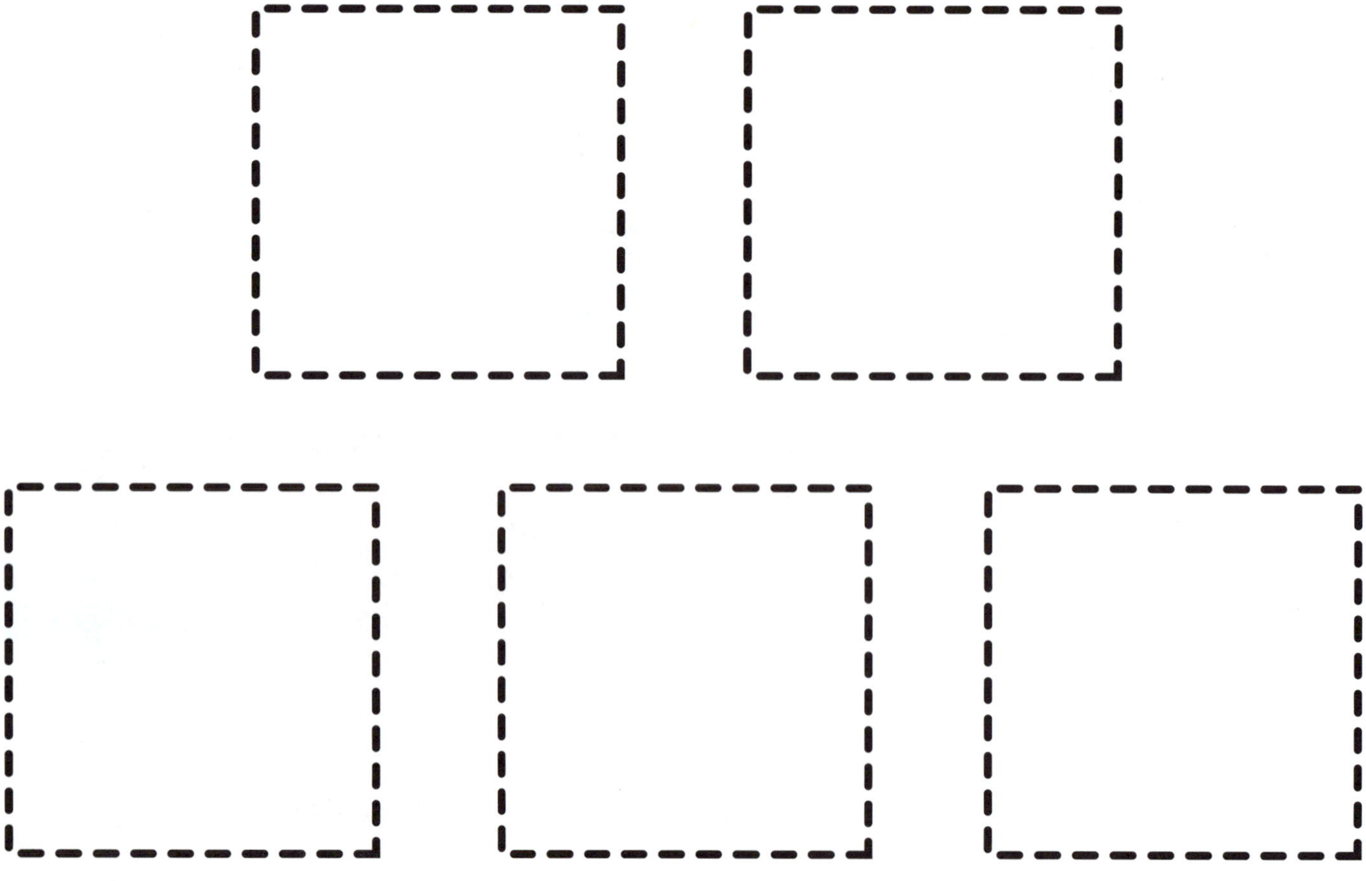

Color the '**square**' shapes to create a path across the page.

Complete the character.

Trace & color the shape.

Draw a line while connecting the 'star' shapes to find your way across the maze.

Complete the character.

Trace & color the shape.

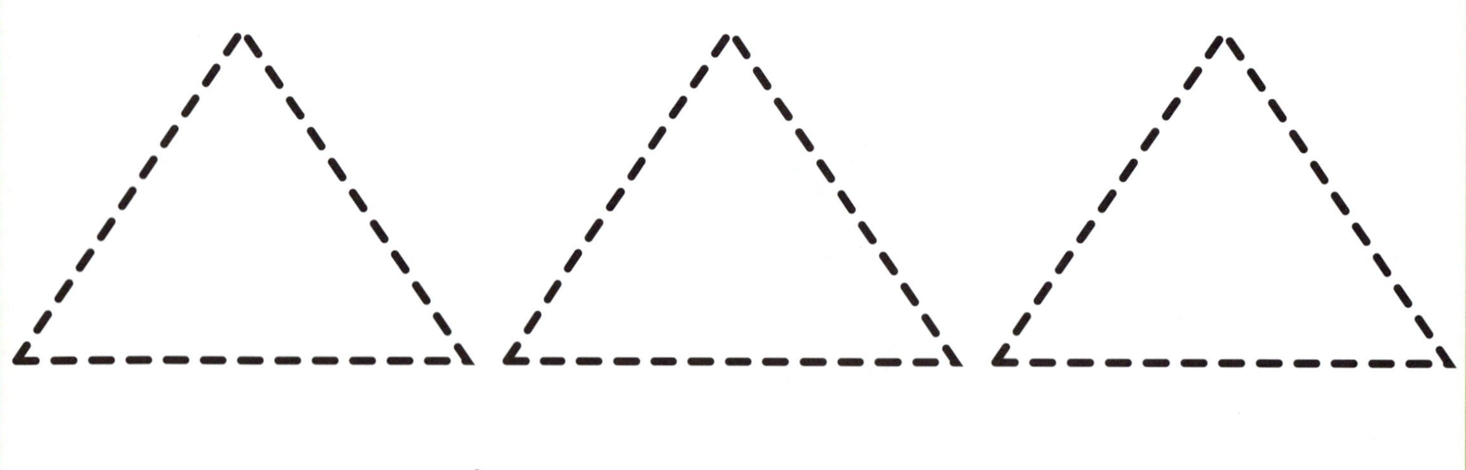

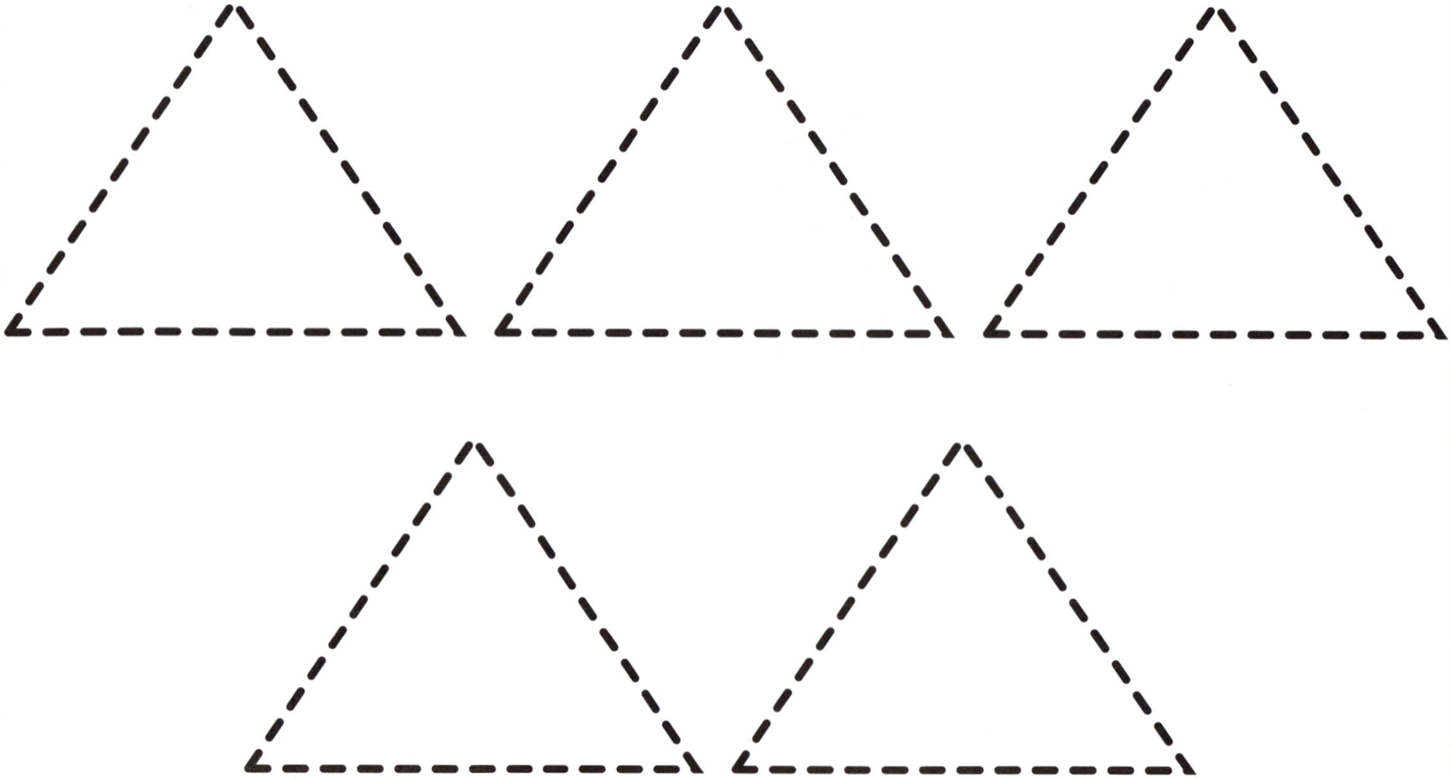

Color the '**triangle**' shapes to create a path across the page.

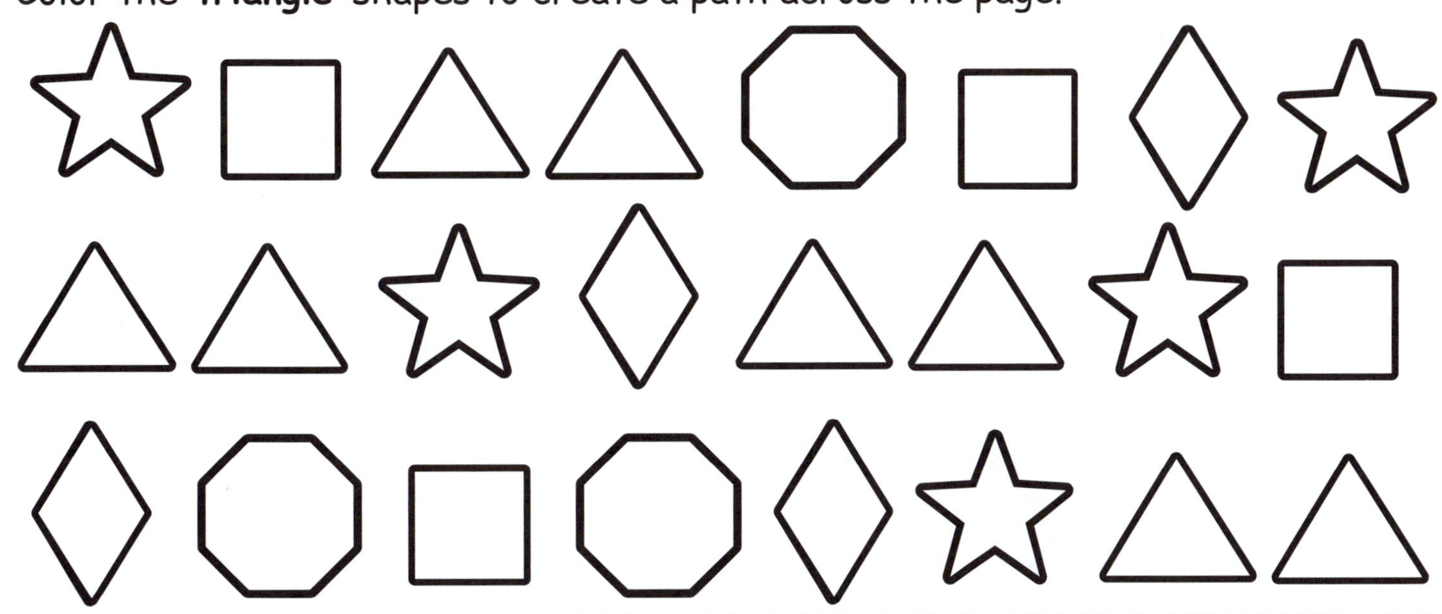

Complete the character.

Connect the dots starting with 'A,' connect the dots starting with '1' and then color the picture.

Connect the dots starting with 'A' then color the picture.

Connect the dots starting with 'A,' connect the dots starting with '1' and then color the picture.

Connect the dots starting with 'A,' connect the dots starting with '1' and then color the picture.

Connect the dots starting with 'A' and then color the picture.

Connect the dots starting with 'A,' connect the dots starting with '1' and then color the picture.

Connect the dots starting with 'A,' connect the dots starting with '1' and then color the picture.

Connect the dots starting with 'A' then color the picture.

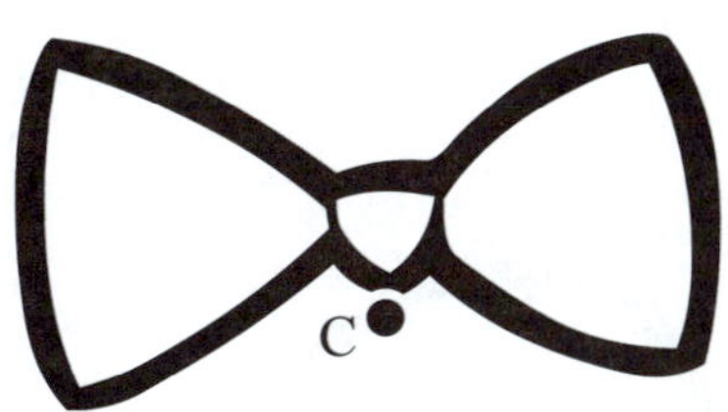

Color the things that are '**circle**' shaped.

Color the things that are '**diamond**' shaped.

Color the things that are '**octagon**' shaped.

Color the things that are '**oval**' shaped.

Color the things that are '**rectangle**' shaped.

Color the things that are '**square**' shaped.

Color the things that are '**star**' shaped.

Color the things that are '**triangle**' shaped.

Circle the 5 things that are different in the 2 pictures.

Circle the 5 things that are different in the 2 pictures.

Draw a line from the shape to the object that matches it.

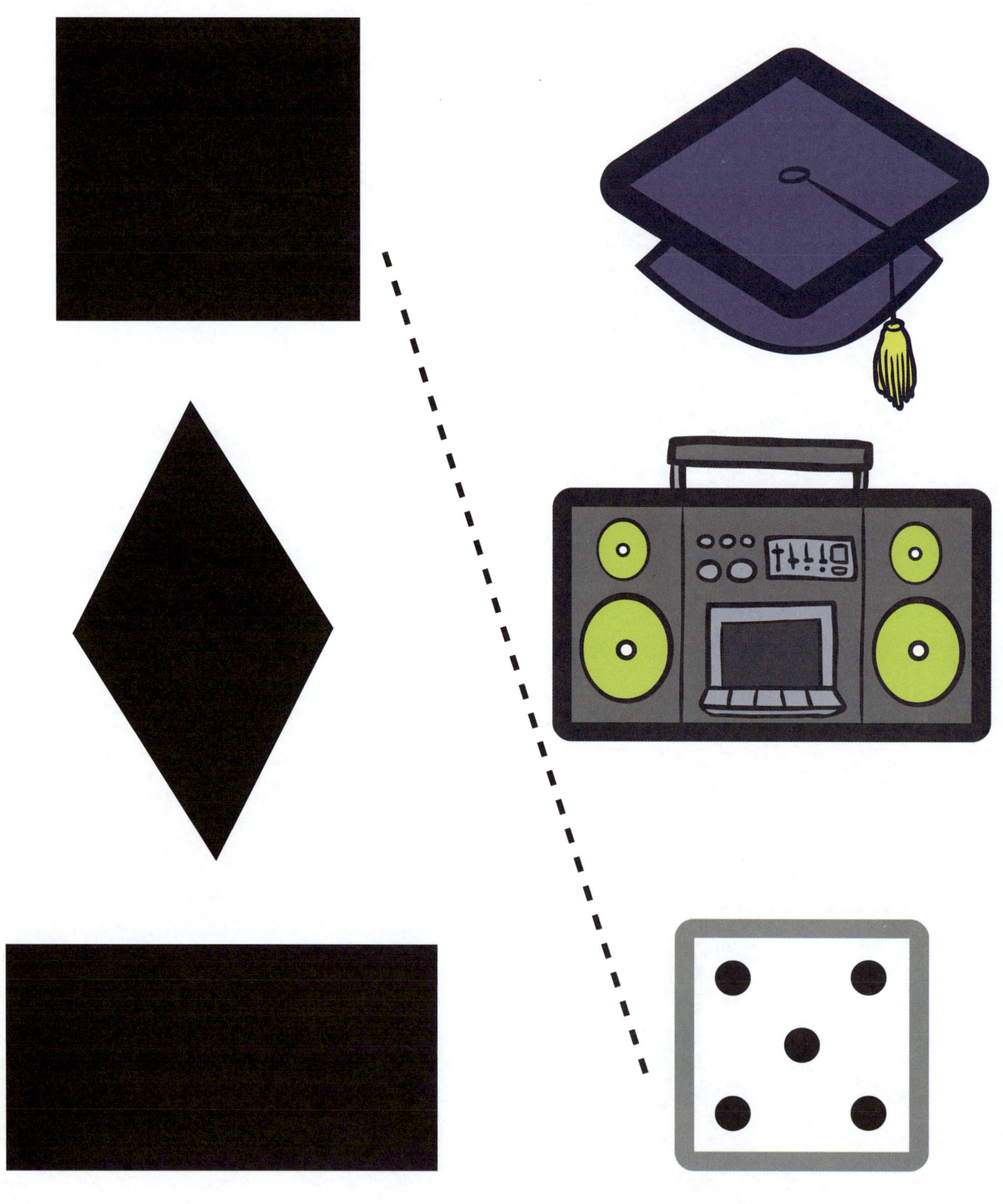

Draw a line from the shape to the object that matches it.

Draw a line from the shape to the object that matches it.

Draw a line from the shape to the object that matches it.

Draw a line from the shape to the object that matches it.

Draw a line from the shape to the object that matches it.

Draw a line from the shape to the object that matches it.

Draw a line from the shape to the object that matches it.

Complete the pattern.

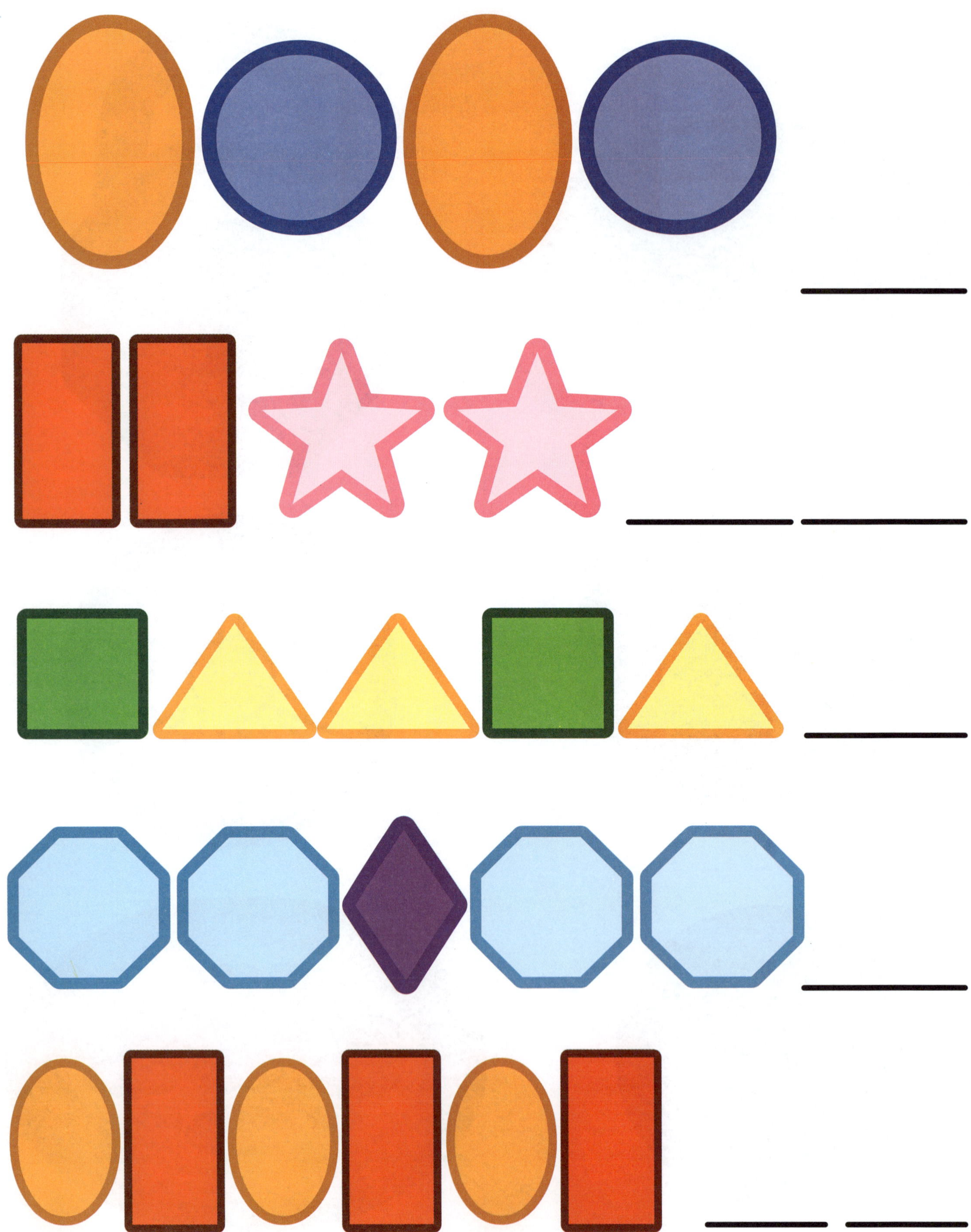

Complete the pattern.

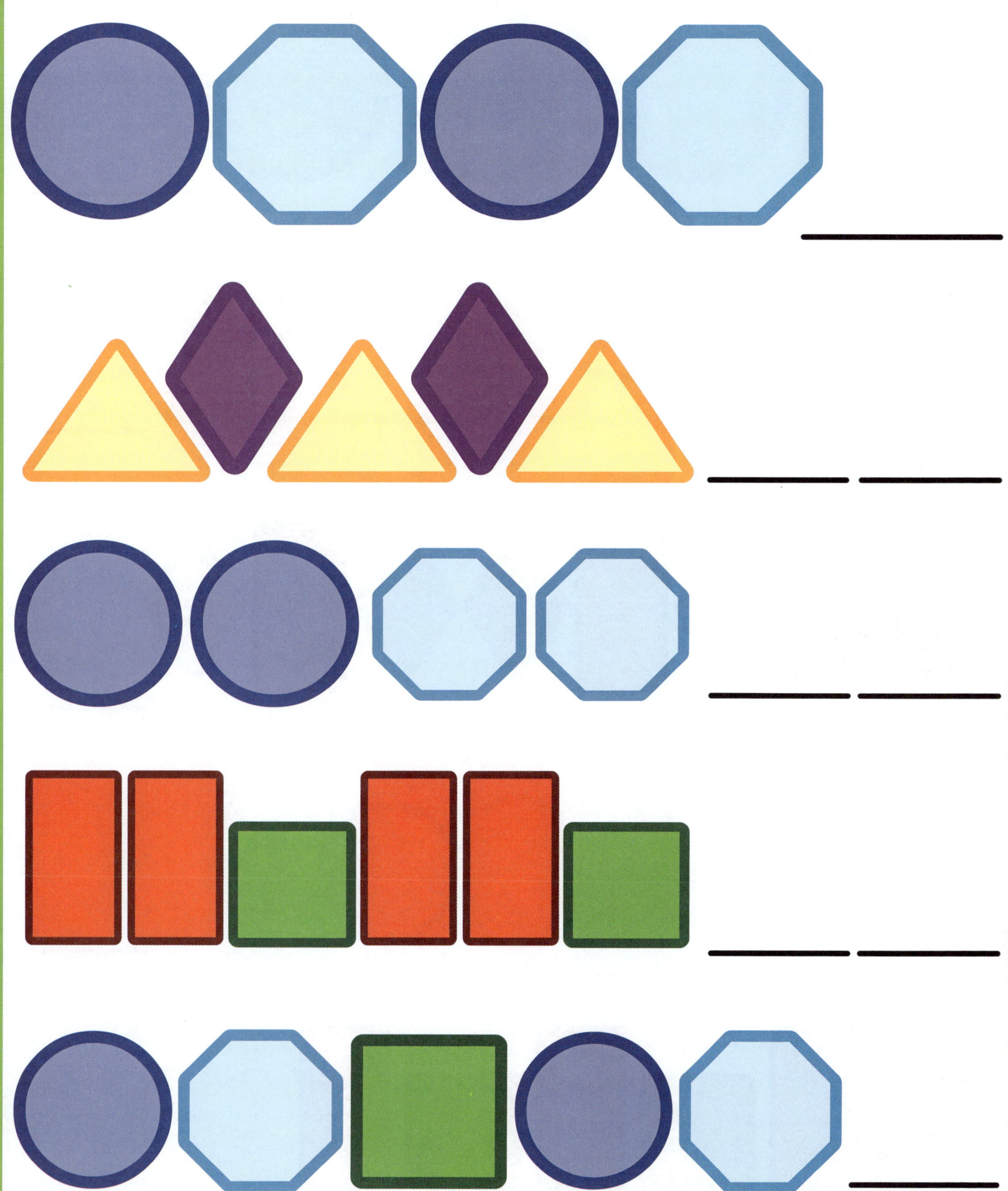

Complete the pattern.

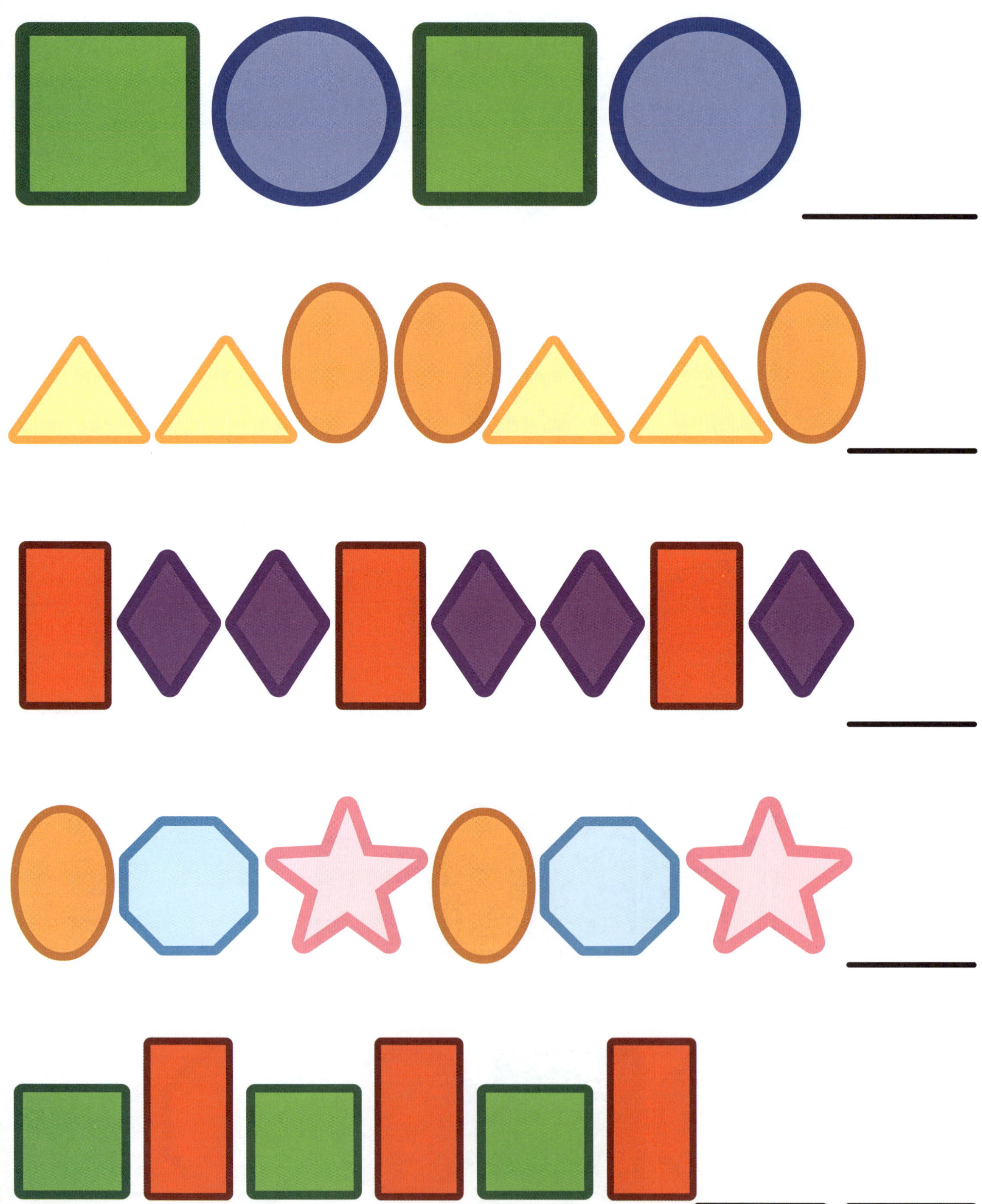

Complete the pattern.

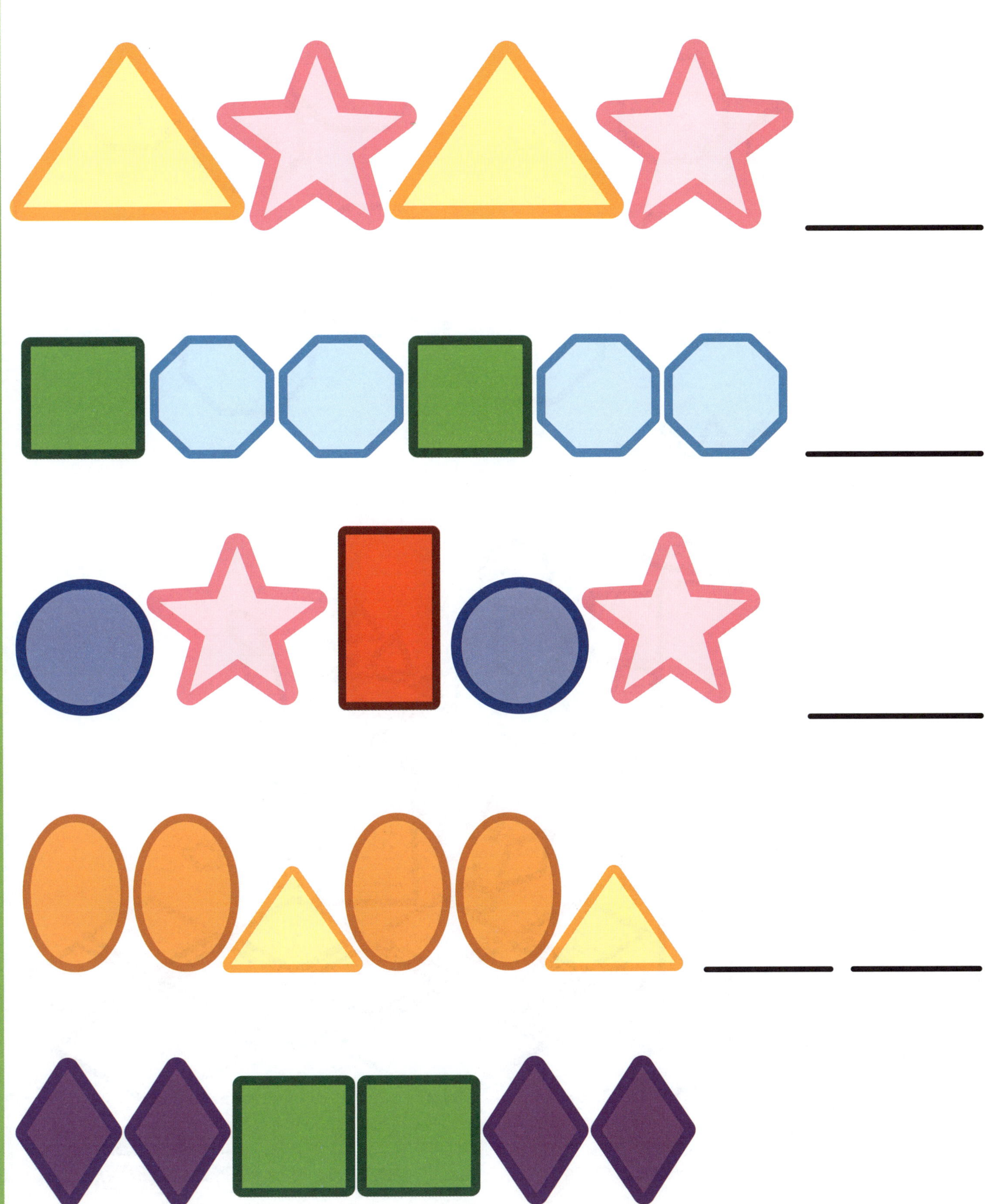

chocolate
chocolate

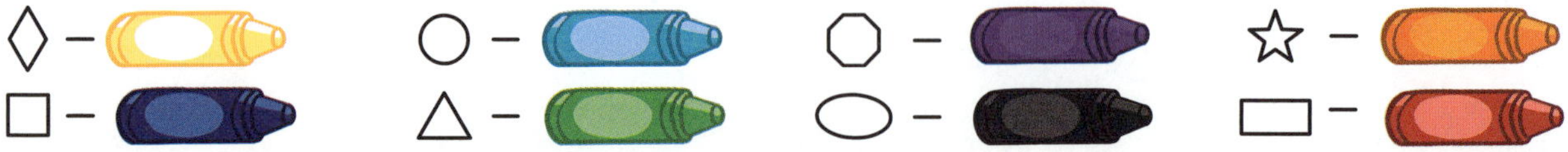

Meet the
Colors™

Color the objects red.

Color the objects orange.

Color the objects yellow.

Color the objects green.

Color the objects blue.

FINISH

Color the objects purple.

Color the objects black.

Color the objects white.

Color the things that are purple.

Color the things that are red.

Color the things that are white.

Color the things that are yellow.

Color the things that are black.

Color the things that are blue.

Color the things that are green.

Color the things that are orange.

Color by Numbers: 1-green 2-purple 3-black 4-brown

Color by Numbers: 1-orange 2-white 3-brown 4-yellow

Color by Numbers: 1-purple 2-green 3-blue 4-yellow

1 2 3 4

Color by Numbers: 1-red 2-green 3-brown 4-blue

Color by Numbers: 1-black 2-brown 3-orange 4-yellow

Color by Numbers: 1-yellow 2-red 3-brown 4-orange

Color by Numbers: 1-black 2-grey 3-blue 4-pink

1 2 3 4

Color by Numbers: 1-blue 2-red 3-green 4-yellow

Circle the 5 things that are different in the 2 pictures.

Circle the 5 things that are different in the 2 pictures.

Color and complete the pattern.

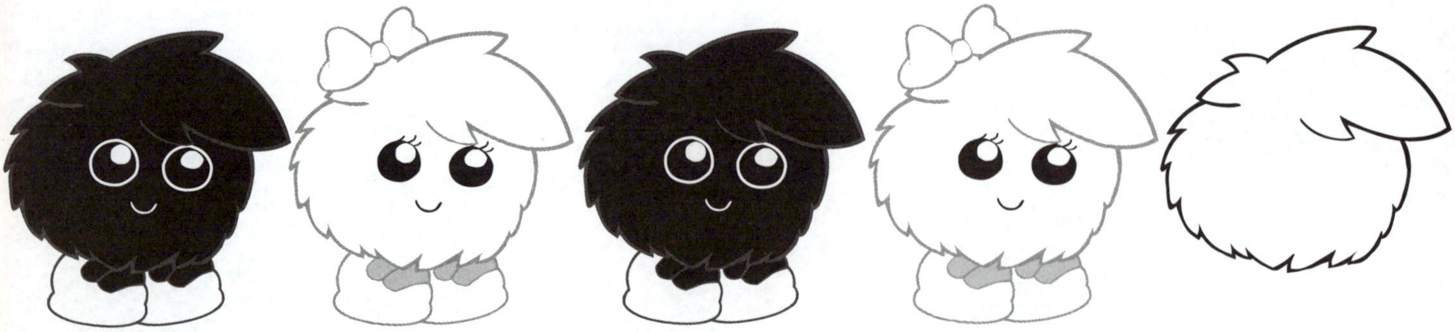

Black White Black White

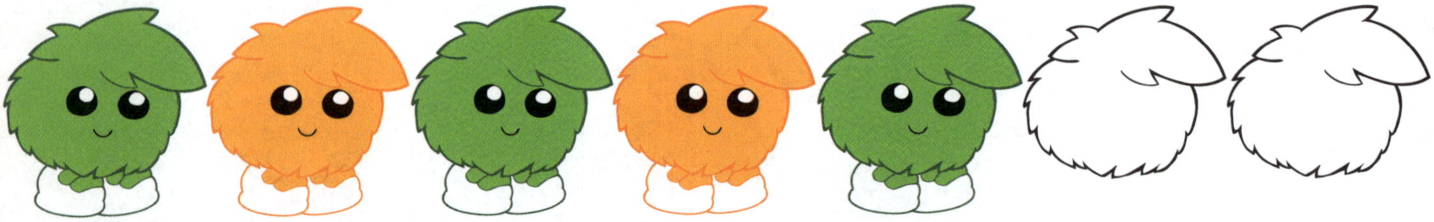

Green Orange Green Orange Green

Purple Purple Red Red Purple Purple

Yellow Yellow Purple Purple Yellow Yellow

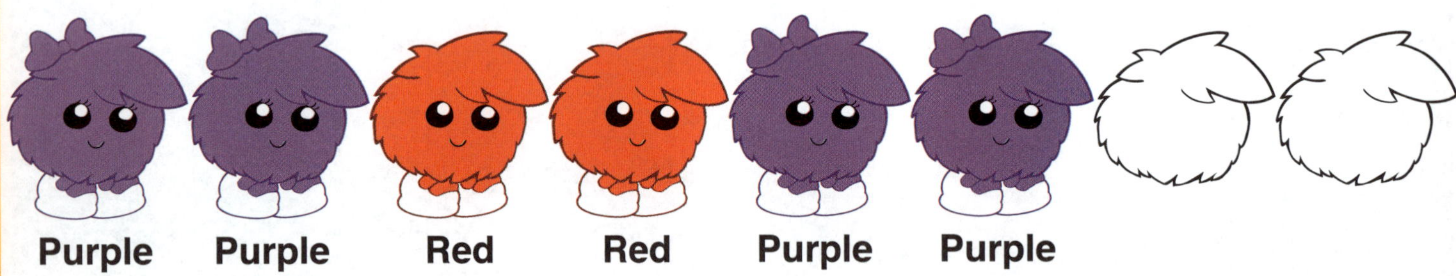

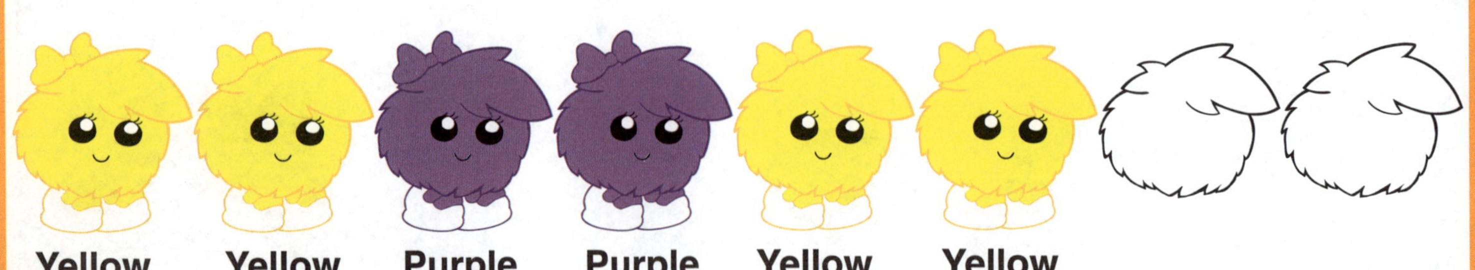

Color and complete the pattern.

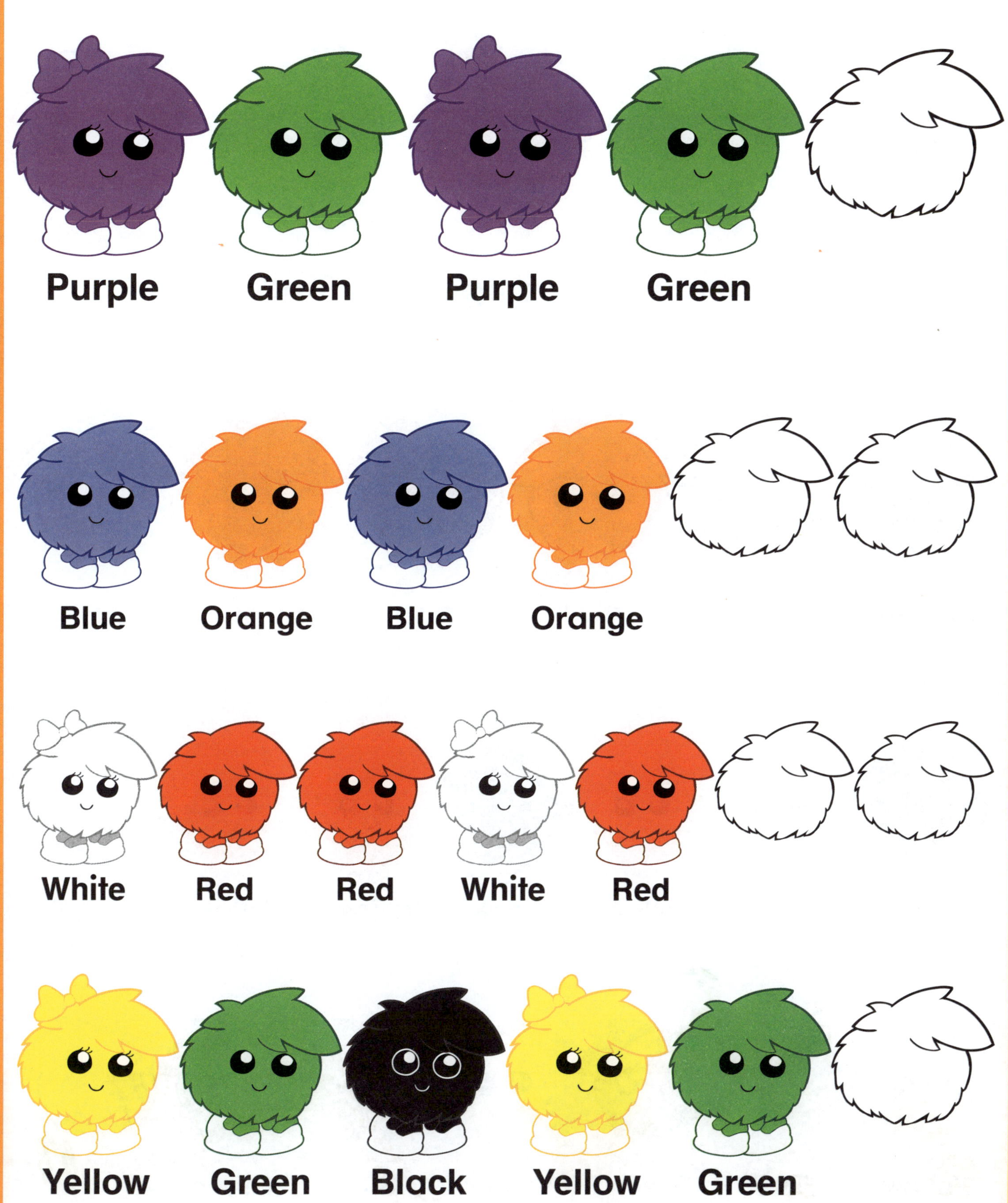

Color and complete the pattern.

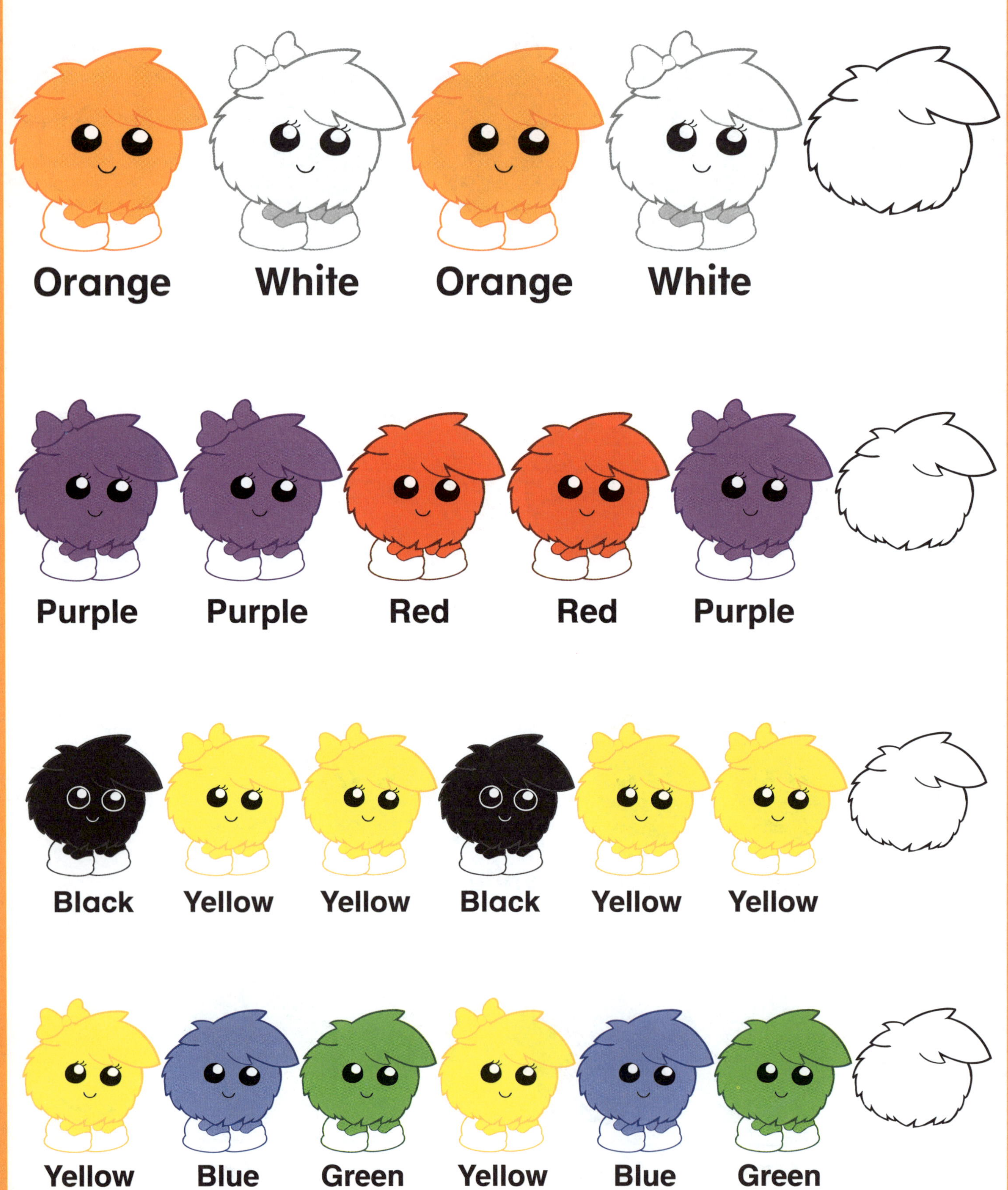

Color and complete the pattern.

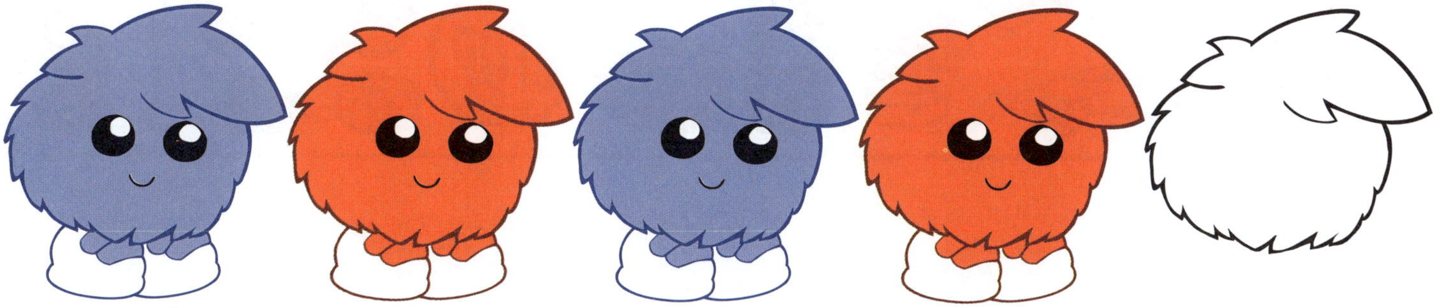

Blue Red Blue Red

Green Green Black Black Green

Orange Purple Purple Orange Purple Purple

Yellow White Red Yellow White Red

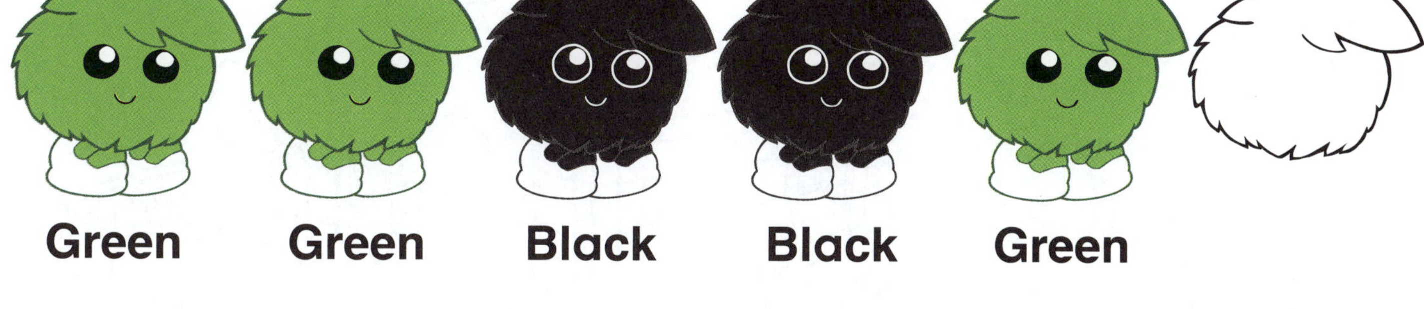

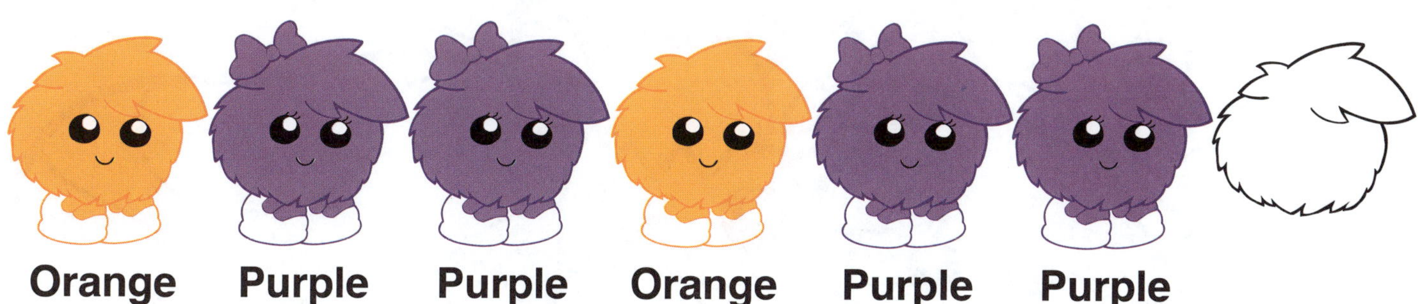

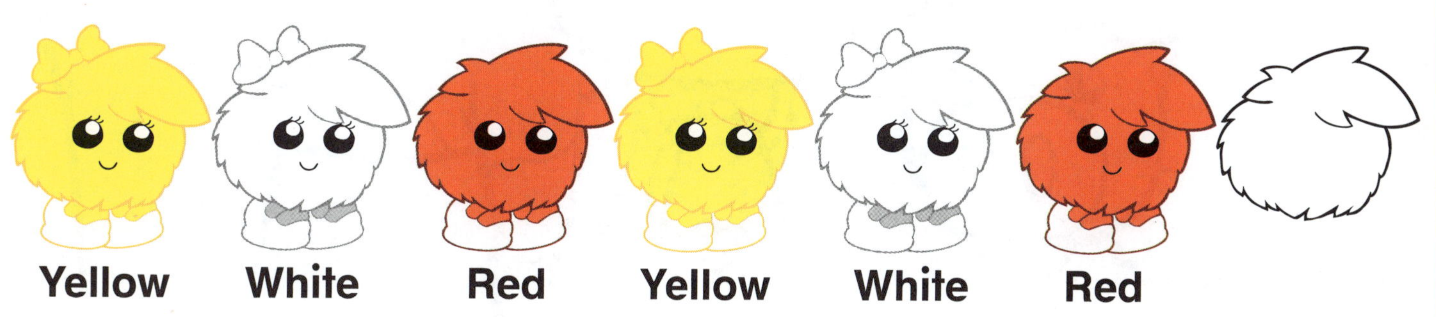

Find these red objects in the picture and color them red:

Find these orange objects in the picture and color them orange:

Find these yellow objects in the picture and color them yellow:

Find these green objects in the picture and color them green:

Find these blue objects in the picture and color them blue:

Find these purple objects in the picture and color them purple:

Find these black objects in the picture and color them black:

Magic Shop

Find these white objects in the picture and color them white:

HEALTH FAIR

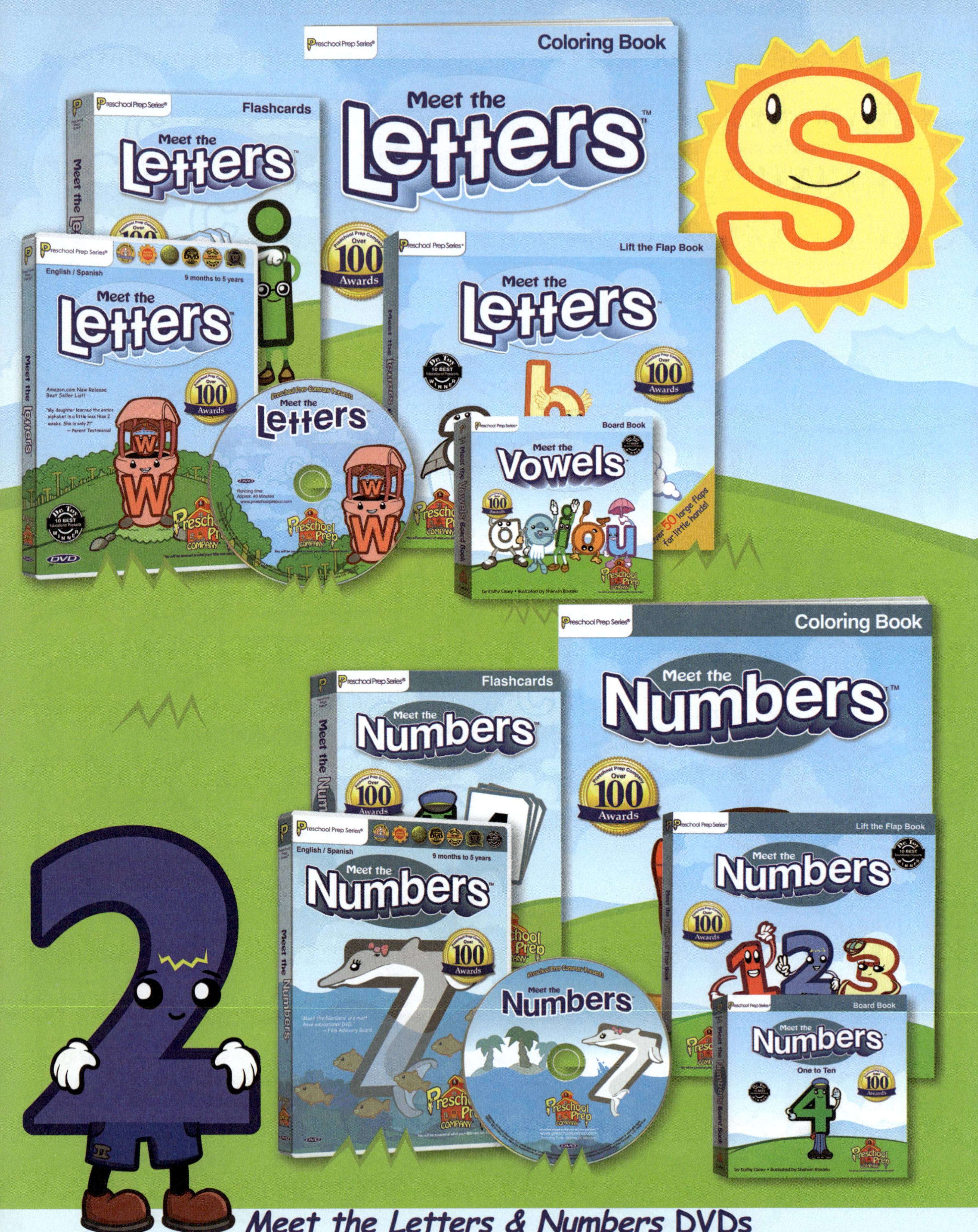

Meet the Letters & Numbers DVDs

Easy Reader Books • Coloring Books • Workbooks • Flashcards

Lift the Flap & Board Books • Apps • eBooks • Video Downloads

Preschool Prep Series
Coloring Book
Meet the Shapes
Flashcards
Meet the Shapes
Over 100 Awards
English / Spanish
9 months to 5 years
Meet the Shapes
Lift the Flap Book
Meet the Shapes
Board Book
Meet the Shapes
Coloring Book
Meet the Colors
Flashcards
Meet the Colors
English / Spanish
9 months to 5 years
Meet the Colors
Lift the Flap Book
Meet the Colors
Board Book
Meet the Colors